THE PARLEY TREE
ARBRE À PALABRES

THE PARLEY TREE
ARBRE À PALABRES

AN ANTHOLOGY OF POETS
FROM FRENCH-SPEAKING AFRICA
AND THE ARAB WORLD

Translated by Patrick Williamson
with Yann Lovelock

Edited and introduced by
Patrick Williamson

with a Preface by
Tahar Bekri

PUBLICATIONS
2012

Published by Arc Publications
Nanholme Mill, Shaw Wood Road
Todmorden, OL14 6DA, UK
www.arcpublications.co.uk

Copyright © individual authors, 2012
Copyright in translations of Mohammed Dib and Tchicaya U Tam'si
© Yann Lovelock, 2012
Copyright in translations of all other poets © Patrick Williamson, 2012
Copyright in the introduction © Patrick Williamson, 2012
Copyright in the present edition © Arc Publications, 2012

Design by Tony Ward
Printed in Great Britain by the MPG Book Group,
Bodmin and King's Lynn

ISBN: 978 1906570 61 3

The publishers are grateful to the authors and, in the case
of previously published works, to their publishers
for allowing their poems to be included in this anthology.

Cover image: Baobab trees © Maniec, 2011

This book is copyright. Subject to statutory exception and to
provisions of relevant collective licensing agreements,
no reproduction of any part may take place without the
written permission of Arc Publications Ltd.

Arc Publications 'Anthologies in Translation'

ACKNOWLEDGMENTS

The poems by Mohammed Dib and Tchicaya U Tam'si have been translated by Yann Lovelock. All other translations are by Patrick Williamson.

All the French poems are reproduced with the kind permission of the author, wherever possible. Although every effort has been made to contact all copyright holders, in certain cases it has not been possible to do so. If you have any information regarding copyright details, please contact the publisher.

Some of the translations in this anthology have appeared in: *Poesie Europe* 1988; *International Poetry Review* 2000 Vol. 26. No. 1; *Les Elephants, or l'infante de Salamanque* (Editions Transignum, 2004); *Fire*, Nos. 29 / 30, March 2008; *Prometeo Latinoamerican Poetry Magazine*, 2008; *Diwan Ifrikiya*, The University of California Book of North African Literature, Poems for the Millennium, volume 4, Nov. 2012, and on the website *Poetryintranslation.org*, 2011.

'Afghanistan' was set to music as 'If Music Were to Die' for a CD by Tahar Bekri & Pol Huellou (Goasco Music, 2011).

CONTENTS

Preface / 9
Introduction / 11

ALGERIA
Mohammed Dib / 19
translated by Yann Lovelock
20 / Migrant • Migrant / 21
20 / La Bête • The beast / 21
22 / Vive plus avant • More than ever alive / 23
22 / La chose • Thing / 23
24 / Le fleuve • River / 25

Habib Tengour / 27
translated by Patrick Williamson
28 / Quatre fois azur et cinq • Four times azure and five / 29
28 / Au bord de l'eau • The water's edge / 29
30 / Le poème • The poem / 31

CAMEROON
Paul Dakeyo / 35
translated by Patrick Williamson
36 / Soweto Soleils Fusillés • Soweto, suns shot down
(extraits)   (extracts) / 37
40 / Le chant de silence • The song of silence
(extraits)   (extracts) / 41

CHAD
Nimrod / 53
translated by Patrick Williamson
54 / Le cri de l'oiseau • The cry of the bird / 55
54 / Tibesti (extraits) • Tibesti (extracts) / 55
56 / Or l'infante de Sala- • Yet the Infanta of Sala-
manque... (extraits)   manca... (extracts) / 57

CONGO BRAZZAVILLE
Alain Mabanckou / 65
translated by Patrick Williamson
66 / Quand le coq annoncera • When the cock announces the
l'aube d'une autre jour   dawn of another day
(extraits)   (extracts) / 67

Tchicaya U Tam'si / 75
translated by Yann Lovelock
76 / Au sommaire d'une • Summary of a passion / 77
passion (extraits)   (extracts)

DEMOCRATIC REPUBLIC OF CONGO
Kama Sywor Kamanda / 83
translated by Patrick Williamson
84 / Dans le silence des cœurs • In the silence of hearts / 85
84 / Le chant de la résistance • The song of resistance / 85
86 / Le chant du destin • The song of destiny / 87
88 / Maisons hantées • Haunted houses / 89
90 / Les roulements du • The beating of the drums / 91
tambour

DJIBOUTI
Abdourahman A. Waberi / 95
translated by Patrick Williamson
96 / Désirs • Desires / 97
96 / Trêve • Truce / 97
96 / Estampes • Engravings / 97
100 / Miniatures nomades • Nomadic miniatures / 101
102 / Sans titre • Untitled / 103
104 / Les dits d'hier • Tales of yesterday / 105

IVORY COAST
Tanella Boni / 109
translated by Patrick Williamson
110 / Le don toujours à venir • The gift still to come
(quatres poèmes)   (four poems) / 111
112 / Gorée île baobab • Gorée baobab island
(quatres poèmes)   (four poems) / 113

LEBANON
Venus Khoury-Ghata / 119
translated by Patrick Williamson
120 / Les Obscurcis (extraits) • The shades (extracts) / 121

MAURITIUS
Edouard Maunick / 129
translated by Patrick Williamson
130 / J'étais un arbre autrefois • I once was a tree / 131

Khal Torabully / 137
translated by Patrick Williamson
138 / Cantate pour l'enfant • Cantata for the child from
de Cana (extrait)   Cana (extract) / 139
138 / Les Indiades, Odes à • Les Indiades, Odes to Pessoa
Pessoa (extrait)   (extract) / 139

140 / Lumière sombre sur l'Aapravasi Ghat (extrait) • Dark light cast on Aapravisi Ghat (extract) / 141
142 / Cale d'étoiles, Coolitude (extraits) • Hold full of stars, Coolitude (extracts) / 143
144 / Dialogue de l'eau et du sel (extraits) • Dialogue of water and salt (extracts) / 145
146 / L'ombre rouge des gazelles (extrait) • The red shadow of gazelles (extract) / 147

MOROCCO
Abdellatif Laâbi / 151
translated by Patrick Williamson

152 / Table rase petite (extraits) • Small clean slate (extracts) / 153
154 / Les épaules et le fardeau (extraits) • Shoulders and the burden (extracts) / 155

SENEGAL
Babacar Sall / 163
translated by Patrick Williamson

164 / Le lit de sable (extraits) • Bed of sand (extracts) / 165

Amadou Lamine Sall / 173
translated by Patrick Williamson

174 / Mon pays n'est pas un pays mort • My country is not a dead country / 175

TUNISIA
Tahar Bekri / 181
translated by Patrick Williamson

182 / Afghanistan • Afghanistan / 183
186 / Ombre • Shade / 187
186 / Songe à Trieste • Dream at Trieste / 187
188 / Le pêcheur de lunes • The Fisherman of Moons / 189

Shams Nadir / 195
translated by Patrick Williamson

196 / L'Autre Sindabad (extraits) • The other Sindbad (extracts) / 197
202 / Echos de l'Isla-Negra • Echoes of Isla Negra / 203

Amina Saïd / 205
translated by Patrick Williamson

206 / "chaque jour le soleil…" • "each day the sun…" / 207
208 / "désormais les mères…" • "the mothers sleep…" / 209
212 / "depuis le lieu natal…" • "from our birth place…" / 213

About the translators / 217

PREFACE

Poetry is clearly one of the major forms of literary expression in both Africa and the Arab World. This anthology, which does not pretend to be exhaustive, endeavours to provide the reader with a glimpse of the most representative voices of the poetic movements, and generations, in the French-speaking countries of these two regions. Such a project is aimed primarily at doing away with the divisions and distinctions between countries of the same continent: Africa. For it is an anomaly to separate North Africa from Sub-Saharan Africa. Similarly, some African countries are also part of the Arab world. International literary and poetry festivals increasingly show the inherent complicity and shared concerns among poets of these southern countries, bridging the artificial divisions generated more by specialised university studies than rooted in fact. The poets themselves have long wished to be associated with common threads and to escape artificial and suspect pigeon-holing, which has long been imposed by fairly reductive historical literary divisions. It is time to knock these down.

We believe that this project could open up a new approach to the poetry of these countries. The French-language poetry of the countries included in this anthology is clearly only one dimension of an overall poetic landscape shared with other national languages: Arabic, Fula, Bambara, Berber, Wolof, and many more. But this poetry, written in French for evident historical reasons, has been confirmed over at least the past half-century as poetry of great literary quality that has won international acclaim. In our view, it would be of great interest for an English-speaking public to discover or better understand this poetry, which has given regular proof of its vitality and presence.

Tahar Bekri
Poet, Maître de Conférences,
Université de Paris X- Nanterre

Why an anthology of French-speaking poetry from Africa and the Arab world? Through chance at the outset, during a meeting with Tahar Bekri, I mentioned that work from these regions warranted greater attention and this led to more prolonged discussion on the matter. We ended up deciding to embark on an anthology of work which, to date, cannot be found on the shelves, a volume which aims to bring together writers (contemporary for the most part) from both Africa and the Arab world, in order to explore what they have in common and what sets them apart. As my recent trawl through a library showed, most anthologies focus on one or other region, with Congolese, Senegalese or Insular poetry shelves quite separate from Tunisian, Algerian, or Lebanese writing, or poets of the Mediterranean Rim, for example.

The Parley Tree aims to present English-speaking readers with material that will enable them to appreciate the wealth of poetry in the French language from the African continent and its outlying areas, and serve as a point of departure to explore the writers in more detail. The work in this anthology reflects the social, political and cultural events that have marked the history of these regions, notably the passage from colonialism to independence – in Algeria, Morocco and Tunisia, subject to monarchical or dictatorial regimes (prior to the Arab Spring and current transition) on the one hand, and in countries such as Chad, Congo Brazzaville, or Democratic Republic of the Congo, where internal and ethnic conflict has remained rife, on the other. In both regions, the poetry reflects the scars of war, man's cruelty to man (see Tanella Boni), and the best way forward to reconciliation. Note, in particular, Paul Dakeyo's poem about Soweto and revolt (p. 37), Mabanckou ("they wounded the ventricles / of the motherland", p. 71), Kamanda's song of resistance (p. 85), and Bekri's poem about the ravages of war in Afghanistan (p. 183). We also see a number of references to Gorée Island in Senegal, a symbol of the Atlantic slave trade.

We considered that poets from the French Antilles formed a separate strand, but we did include poets from Mauritius given that, like the Arab world, its history was also made of various migratory waves and the cultural mosaic prevalent on the island (with Creole, English, and French as languages) reflects the diversity and the discourse of identity. Looking at Negro African poetry, I did not include Léopold Sédar Senghor, as his often theoretical work is widely translated and commented on already. It should be noted, though, that he was one of the originators of the concept of Négritude, viewed as both the literary and artistic expression of the black African experience and, simultaneously, an ideological reaction against French colonialism and a defence of African culture. The concept deeply influenced the French-speaking black and Arab world and many poets in this anthology have paid homage to him. But Tchicaya U Tam'si, like many other poets, took a different attitude to the principles of Négritude, notably stating "every negro poet is not automatically a Négritude poet". This stance fits well with the texts presented in this anthology: not theory, but men. Tchicaya U Tam'si again: "I come from an ethnic group, I have a nationality, I am African, I write. In the end there is no ethnic, or national or African writing… I am a writer."

With regard to the French language, in the Maghreb region there has always been very down-to-earth poetry in Berber or Arab dialect, and also elaborate poetry, which has constantly celebrated mankind's need for the absolute and divine mystery, in classical Arab. But the latter has remained a language for the élite and perhaps this explains, in part, why many of the recent generation of poets from this region have written in French, finding that they can use the colonial language as a means of reaching a wider audience, be this Maghreb or western. Their predecessors prior to the 1940s, however, were reluctant to write in what they viewed as a pale imitation of pure poetry, and this is a difference between North Africa and the rest of the continent, which adopted French as a *lingua franca* well before this date (note the congregations of African and West Indian writers in pre-war Paris).

Poetry in native African languages existed long before poetry in French arrived, and there are many such poems that merit being collected and saved for future generations. African poetry in French, although it will always lack some of its authenticity when written in a tongue foreign to the continent, reflects all the real contradictions, tensions and internal conflicts that African people are subject to. In poetry, one has to go beyond the literal interpretation to find the sub-text, and this is especially true for poetry that is written in a language that is not the poet's mother tongue. We considered that the writers represented in this anthology belong to a school of French-African, rather than purely African, poetry, owing to the authors having been steeped in French literary traditions as well as those inherent to the continent.

This French-African poetry harbours, in addition to the classic themes of man's destiny, a quest for irrefutable proof of origins, an affirmation of belonging, – "We seek our roots / Like others seek hidden truths" (Kamanda, p. 91) – a quest for an identity that the colonial powers had more or less eradicated and caricatured through official histories and ethnology. In cultural exile, writers often feel they are no longer rooted in their own national culture. These poets want to regain control of their destiny and not to be tied to the history of another, foreign, country. Everything converges towards the same aspirations. African poetry in French is a witness to the assumed tearing apart of the culture, to the quest for a historical underpinning of the collective 'me' lost in anonymity.

The African continent is full of paradoxes and contrasts, and artistic expression is wide-ranging and takes many forms, lyric poetry being one of the most prominent. Lyricism here has to be taken in the broadest sense of the term, a poetical style or inspired language expressing innermost feelings through rhythms and images. It is said that most African poets generally attach greater importance to lyrical themes, which are considered to be really poetical, than to revolt and claims, which are often linked to historical circumstances and events. At first glance, the latter predominates with the result that African poetry could appear to be very specific. But other themes soon emerge, notably 'Love' with a capital L. Kama Kamanda's poetry, for example, fervently proclaims the advent of justice, fraternity and love, offering us a humanity that crosses all racial and cultural boundaries. As with other poets here, nostalgia for Africa lies at the heart of poetry which is full of music, thanks to the skilful use of repetitions and inner rhymes.

Tradition, myth, and visceral attachment to ancestral land are major strands in poetry from the continent, whether the poets come from Congo, or from North Africa with its privileged position as a geographical and historical crossroads for numerous cultures. The poetry from the latter region is one of metaphysics, and calls more on the imaginary than on concepts. Metaphysical themes underpin modern post-colonial poetry in both Arabic and, probably to a greater extent, in French, acting as a way of federating people by bringing to the fore all the ancient cultural values (note Shams Nadir in this respect), as if to say "we have a cultural worth strong enough to resist any onslaught". Tahar Bekri's poems, for example, plunge us into the world of exile and memories of the home country. Although references to Arab mythology and poetry of the past mark it out as intellectual, his poetry is a true quest for light and love, with the sea a recurring theme in his work.

Aside from love and revolt, writing from both sides of the Sahara expands on other themes: life, death, childhood, solitude, melancholy. Many commentators either denigrate these universal themes, or are inclined to pigeon-hole the poets from each region or strand, writing solely about the militant aspect of their poetry. But even for those who talk of revolution, the poetry has to be firmly anchored in past and present and open to the modern world.

What might be called 'feminine' poetry is more discreet, more intimate and clearly has a purifying function. Women write about the pain of solitude and anguish and the enduring strength of love, memory and identity, and although their concerns are much the same as those of the males poets, their perspective is uniquely feminine. I am thinking here of Amina Said's poem of the mothers lamenting their dead sons (p. 209), or Tanella Boni's "different skins" (p. 111). This is writing that wants to use poetry to heal wounds, to heal the earth as well as opening the door to new horizons. There is a need to put forward the subjective view of women who, from time immemorial, have been bridled by patriarchal societies. These female poets claim their right to existence and love, and to question the feminine condition and rediscover their bodies; above all they, like men, claim a rightful place in the common fight to establish new, free and fraternal societies.

The "parley tree" (*arbre à palabres*) in Africa has traditionally been the baobab tree. It is a meeting place, a place of discussion, where the people of the village can talk about local issues, politics, etc. It is also a place where children can meet to hear stories read by a village elder. Reading through this anthology, I am struck by the number of references to the baobab, from Maunick ('I once was a tree' p. 131) through U Tam'si, Kama Kamanda, Boni ('Gorée baobab island', p. 113), and Amadou Lamine Sall ("My country is not a nocturnal baobab / blackened grass a cold flower", p. 175).

The baobab as a social institution at the nerve centre of the village is one of the key elements of the cultures that occupy Africa, especially at the frontiers of the Congo. It acts as a federating component for different groups to communicate together, over and above a 'misleading' ethnic and linguistic diversity, enabling them to cohabit, and to settle conflicts and differences. Discussions serve as a link between the living and the dead;

conflicts are resolved under the watchful eyes of ancestors. Clearly, this tree not only symbolises the common threads between the various cultures of the continent, but also reconciliation through the idea of parley or discussion.

Poetry from Africa and the Arab world is impregnated with oral tradition, and participants in the "court" of the parley tree (which anyone can ask to sit) are the epitome of eloquence, using proverbs, metaphors, fables and poems, which are often presented with admirable dexterity. As a point of passage between past and present, and a link between the profane and the sacred, the parley tree reflects the essences and depths of Africa in all its forms. I hope that the poetry presented in this anthology does likewise.

*

I would like to thank all the poets that agreed to appear in this anthology, and who waived the translation rights to their texts, notably Tahar Bekri, who also helped with the selection.

I would also like to thank: the publishing houses Editions l'Harmattan and Editions de la Différence for graciously waiving their rights; Yann Lovelock for his translations of Mohammed Dib and Tchicaya U'Tam'si; Maureen Smith and Philip Wilson for their reading and editorial help in the early stages of the project; and last but not least, Angela Jarman and Tony Ward of Arc Publications for taking on the project and for their editing work.

Patrick Williamson

ALGERIA

MOHAMMED DIB

MOHAMMED DIB was born at Tlemcen in 1920. After working as a teacher (prior to the Second World War), he joined the paper *Alger républicain*, which he quit in 1951. He was expelled from Algeria in 1959 and later settled in the western Paris suburbs. His first work on French soil, *Ombre Gardienne* (1961) was warmly received by Louis Aragon and André Malraux. A professor at the University of California in 1974 and winner of the Prix Mallarmé for *L'enfant-jazz* in 1998, Mohammed Dib's poetic universe resembles, on more than one count, an unexplored, underground, black continent. His last collections were *Le cœur insulaire* (2000) and *L.A. Trip* (2003), a novel in verse. Dib died at La Celle Saint-Cloud, near Paris, in 2003.

MIGRANT

Ce qu'il a. Avoir quitté.
Etre allé ailleurs prendre
acte de son existence.

Et rien: serments jurés,
souvenirs, mises en garde
qu'on ne foule aux pieds.

Migrant, le serait-on
de seconde main déjà.
Toujours aller prendre acte.

La vie, une migration
serait-elle de dixième main.
Ou de millième main.

    L.A. Trip – a novel in verse (Editions de La Différence, 2003)

LA BÊTE

Une bête vint le chercher.
Il eut moins peur que de rester.

Ils eurent la porte à passer.
La porte en plus de la nuit.

Le garçon ferma les yeux.
Les mots ne parlèrent plus.

Quelque chose sur la route
Les prit alors en pitié.

    L'enfant-Jazz (Editions de La Différence, 1998)

MIGRANT

What he has. Having left.
Gone elsewhere to take
note of his existence.

And nothing: oaths sworn,
memories, told not to
be trampled under foot.

Migrant, you'd be
second-hand already.
Always about to take note.

Life, it would be a
tenth-hand migration.
Or a thousandth-hand.

THE BEAST

The beast came to get him.
He was less afraid than to remain.

There was the door to pass.
The door more than the night.

The boy shut his eyes.
Words no longer spoke.

Along the road something
Took care of them in pity.

VIVE PLUS AVANT

je m'habille
seulement de seins
d'épaules de hanches

blanc cataclysme
j'abreuve en moi la bête
fauve et tranquille

je l'use de même
bouche contre bouche
et en fais une eau

ni geste ni parole
encore moins le regard
moins la fable

sauf la bête
qui me garde au centre
et lessive à grand feu

    Feu beau feu (Editions de La Différence, 1979)

LA CHOSE

On ne savait quoi
Une chose, dit-il.

De ces comment dire
Choses tranquilles.

De ces choses calmes
Qui restent sur place.

Lui aussi restait là.
Elle ne le savait pas.

MORE THAN EVER ALIVE

I dress myself
only in breasts
in shoulders in hips

a white cataclysm
I water the beast in me
wild and tame

I use it the same
mouth to mouth
and turn it to water

no gesture no word
still less a look
less fable

than beast
that keeps me encompassed
and launders me in fire

THING

No knowing.
A thing, he said.

One of those sort of
Well behaved things.

Those peaceful things
That stay put.

He stayed too.
It didn't know.

Il dit: bonjour.
Il mit un genou à terre.

Le garçon attendit.
Il mit l'autre à terre.

Puis il n'attendit rien,
Les genoux à terre.

    L'enfant-Jazz (Editions de la Différence, 1998)

LE FLEUVE

Le clair de lustre était pour lui.
Rien pour la mère assise là-bas.
Elle, comme au bord d'un fleuve.

Ne parlant pas. Attendant. Assise.
Que le fleuve eût fini de passer.
Et lui, ses paupières battirent.

Le fleuve qui sans jamais passer.
Le sommeil qui sans jamais passer.
Lui non plus sans jamais passer.

Il ferma les yeux. Le fleuve déborda.
N'en finir pas de déborder. Et quoi?
La mère était toujours assise là-bas.

    L'enfant-Jazz (Editions de la Différence, 1998)

Hallo, he said,
One knee to earth.

The boy waited.
Put down the other.

Then waited for nothing,
Both knees on the earth.

RIVER

The light's glint was for him.
Nothing for the mother seated there.
She, as if at the riverside.

Not talking. Waiting. Seated.
For the river to cease passing.
And he, his eyelids fluttered.

Passing without end, the river.
Sleep passing without end.
Passing without end, he too.

He shut his eyes. The river overflowed.
Overflowed without cease. And then?
The mother seated there as ever.

HABIB TENGOUR

Habib Tengour was born at Mostaganem in 1947. Poet, writer and anthropologist, he has constantly moved back and forth between France and Algeria. Tengour has published both prose, notably *Gens de Mosta* (1997), which won the Prix Afrique Méditerranéenne / Maghreb, ADELF 1997, and *Le maître de l'heure*, and poetry, including *Traverser, Gravité de l'ange* and *La sandale d'Empédocle*. Tengour currently works as a sociologist in the Essone, near Paris.

QUATRE FOIS AZUR ET CINQ

Sable pierre ou minéral c'est un bleu outre-mer
que la mémoire accroche à ses rayons
frêle trace d'un campement
pour traverser nos vies disposées en miroir
à l'heure où les hachures s'estompent dans le gris
et le ciel stérile de couleurs

Le voyage tu ne peux pas le raconter
ce goût de cendre quand les mots fusent
ni la joie éblouissante au moment d'accoster

Longtemps j'ai fixé la ligne
cherchant obstinément un repère

Pâle à l'instant des comptes ton livre sur l'étal
visiblement inquiet
il n'est plus question de fuir

Le spectre est muet
il ne livrera pas son secret avant le chant du coq
l'angoisse qui circule dans la nuit n'est pas fatale
même si la peur hante les étoiles

Dans la chambre l'aurore répand des paillettes d'or
aussi l'azur vient boire dans tes lèvres

    (previously unpublished)

AU BORD DE L'EAU

La mer, tu la regardes et tu cherches
un mot
La vague cogne les récifs

Tu t'éloignes du bord
                              Ne pas mouiller tes chaussures neuves

FOUR TIMES AZURE AND FIVE

Sand stone or mineral ultramarine blue
memory attaches to its rays
frail trace of a camp
to cross our lives set out in a mirror
just as hachures fade to grey
and the sky is colour sterile

The trip, you cannot tell us about it
this ash taste when words merge
nor the burst of joy when landing

I stared and stared at the line
stubbornly searching for a bearing

Pale at the time of reckoning your book on the stall
visibly unsettled
no longer a question of flight

The spectre is mute
it will not reveal its secret before cock-crow
the anguish that roams at night is not fatal
even though fear haunts the stars

In the bedroom, dawn sprinkles its gold sequins
and azure drinks from your lips

THE WATER'S EDGE

Sea, you look at it you search for
a word
Waves strike the reefs

You move back from the edge
                        Don't get your new shoes wet

L'eau de mer attaque le cuir
L'état de tes chaussures te préoccupe
presque autant que le mot qui se dérobe
avec l'écume

Ton œil gobe le large
et tu te sens satisfait
peut-être un peu inquiet à cause des giclées
des crevasses
Tu n'es pas équipé pour la ballade...

    (previously unpublished)

LE POÈME

L'œil pèse sur le cercle de lumière
A peine éveillé le regard titube
S'accroche à la pierre éclaboussée
Frémissement à l'attente du bleu

La figure de style du poète obscur
encerclée
prend forme le moment venu
Etrangement
se précise au pied du lit

Obscurité de l'heure médiane
à un tournant envisageable

Ces gens qui évitent de te saluer
maladroitement continuent leurs rêves nocturnes

Dans l'urgence le poème se fragmente
ce qu'il dit sans effort le moment le capte

    (previously unpublished)

Seawater ruins leather
The state of your new shoes worries you
almost as much as the word that slips away
with the foam

Your eye swallows up the wide expanse of sea
and you feel satisfied
maybe slightly uneasy on account of the spray
or cracks
You are not kitted out for a walk...

THE POEM

The eye weighs heavy on the circle of light
barely awake the look reels
clings to splattered stone
quivering in expectation of the blue

The stylistic device of the obscure poet
encircled
takes shape when the time comes
Strangely
becomes clear at the foot of the bed

Obscurity of the median hour
at a possible turning point

These people that avoid greeting you
awkwardly continue their night-time dreams

Urgently, the poem fragments
the moment captures what it effortlessly says

CAMEROON

PAUL DAKEYO

PAUL DAKEYO was born in Cameroon in 1948. Founder of the publishing house Editions Silex, he belongs to the second generation of Cameroonian writers that, despite their pessimism, wish to see their country come out of the socio-economic stagnation that followed the first years of independence. Paul Dakeyo, and many others, express the horror of those bloody régimes whose ruthless pursuit of power became a feature of African politics. His poetry denounces injustice and abuse of every kind, and calls for reconciliation worldwide. His collections of note include *Barbelés du matin*, *Chant d'accusation*, *Soweto: soleils fusillés* and *Les ombres de la nuit*. He is currently working on a book in honour of Nelson Mandela.

SOWETO SOLEILS FUSILLÉS (extraits)

Ma colère
Comme de grands vents
Qui rythment la marche
De ma patrie levée
Et mon peuple debout
Face à la nuit rageuse
Mon peuple debout
Comme l'écume de nos souffrances
Comme la tempête dure.

Et nos martyrs
Qui ne sont pas morts
Nos martyrs
Qui sont dans mon chant
Dans l'air la mer
Comme un volcan furieux.

Je te porterai sur ma terre
A peine sèche de larmes
Je te porterai parmi les fleurs
Le pollen le volcan pur
Je te porterai comme un soleil
Le long de la marche finale
Je te porterai amoureusement
Jusque dans le réveil
De ma terre lointaine
Jusque dans le silence débridé
De nos latitudes solitaires
Je te porterai.

Le temps est long
Et longue la marche
L'attente de l'étreinte
Chaude du grand jour

SOWETO, SUNS SHOT DOWN (extracts)

My anger
The high winds
That punctuate the march
My homeland in revolt
My people rising up
Against raging night
My people rising up
Ferment of our suffering
The raging storm

And our martyrs
That are not dead
Our martyrs
That are in my song
In the air the sea
Like a volcano in fury

I will carry you over my land
Barely dry from tears
I will carry you among the flowers
Pollen the pure volcano
I will carry you a sun
All through the final march
I will carry you lovingly
Even in the stirring
Of my faraway country
Even in the unbridled silence
Of our solitary corner of the world
I will carry you

Time hangs heavy
The march drags on
Waiting for the warm
Embrace of the great day

L'attente de l'amour
Et des moissons futures
Le temps est long
Et longue la marche
Dans la nuit
Seule et froide.

Nous marcherons sur les ronces
Avec notre insoumission
A l'ordre
Avec notre insoumission
A l'espace carcéral
Notre insoumission finale
A la nuit
Jusqu'à la liberté.

Et au bout de la marche
Nous nous lierons d'amitié
Avec le jour intime
Avec le feu, l'air, l'eau
Et le matin plus clair
Comme une étreinte chaude
Qui sonde le vent virginal
De nos géographies parallèles
Nous nous lierons d'amitié
Comme nos bras qui enlacent
inlassablement le temps.

Alors nous sortirons de l'exil
Comme un essaim d'abeilles
Comme un raz de marée
Qui reflue a l'horizon
Écorché par le vent
Comme autant d'étoiles hissées
Au beau milieu du ciel
Nous sortirons de l'exil
Comme un volcan déchaîné.

Waiting for love
And harvests to come
Time hangs heavy
The march drags on
In the night
Cold and alone

We will walk on thorns
In insubordination
To order
In insubordination
To prison space
Our final insubordination
In the night
Till freedom come

And when the march ends
We will strike up a friendship
With the intimacy of day
With fire, water, air
And a brighter morning
A warm embrace
That probes the virgin wind
Of our parallel geographies
We will strike up friendship
Our arms that untiringly
Embrace time

So we will emerge from exile
A swarm of bees
A tidal wave
That ebbs to the horizon
Flayed by wind
Like so many stars hoisted
To the very centre of the sky
We will emerge from exile
Like a raging volcano

J'irai te promener
Sur la grève
Le long du littoral
Quand la brise frise
La mer
La mer interminable.

J'irai offrir à l'aube
La dimension de l'amour
Et l'odeur câline
de ton corps frappé
De soleils.

Alors nous irons
Sur le sable
Lisse de ma terre
Seuls dans l'amour
A l'heure où le flux
Berce les récifs élimés
De silences

    Soweto: soleils fusillés (Droite et Liberté, 1977)

LE CHANT DE SILENCE (extraits)

Comme le temps est triste
mais je vais par le passé
remonter les racines
jusqu'à ma terre ténébreuse
où je sème les étoiles
pour célébrer la femme où j'ai mal

Je vais m'asseoir pour longtemps
seul parmi les arbres
et la lave bleue de mon chant
pour hâter le sommeil

I will take you to walk
On the shore
Along the coast
When the breeze skims
The sea
The never-ending sea

I will offer dawn
The magnitude of love
And your snugly
Sun-beaten
Body

And we will go on
Across the smooth sand
Of my land
Alone in love
Just as the incoming tide
Lulls the worn reefs
With silence

THE SONG OF SILENCE (extracts)

These are sad times
but I will return back up
the past to my roots
to my tenebrous country
where I scatter stars
to celebrate the woman where I hurt

I will sit and sit
alone among the trees
the blue lava of my song
to hasten my sleep

Ma fille est là haute
et belle comme la lune
c'est l'été mais que restera-t-il
de la tendresse demain

Tu es partie et j'entre dans le vertige
Tu es partie et je somnanbule
dans tout ce qu'efface
mes gestes lents de désespérance

Tu es la terre qui m'appelle
je sais que la nuit va durer
et que le champs s'effondra
dans chaque mot dans chaque horizon en ruines
que nos vies deviendront un désert

un exil plus profond de nous-mêmes
une tourmente de silence
et de trahison
je sais le signe est vertical
il porte un instant de lumière vraie

plongeons-nous aux méandres de la mémoire
pour mieux nous saisir
images rythmes clartés illuminations
organisation même de l'univers des choses
Mouvement et force inscrits dans les roches de la terre offensée
Nous-mêmes

et je veux écrire pour effacer nos baisers
et je veux écrire pour ne pas mourir
aux pieds de la terre ou j'ai mal
Entassement de rêves sombres
ils ont tué la parole ma parole
et mon coeur qui bat plus vite que l'éclair
ils ont brisé les persiennes closes de ton regard
quand l'aurore nous saisi à la taille

Le passé n'est plus qu'un souvenir
et midi me permet de contempler encore ton
visage

My daughter is here
tall beautiful as the moon
it is summer but what will remain
of tenderness when it has gone

You have left and I feel dizzy
You have left and I sleepwalk
through all that effaces
my slow movements of despair

You are the earth that calls me
I know that night will be long
and the field will cave in
with every word with every horizon in ruins
that our lives will be a wilderness

exile from our deeper selves
a torment of silence
and betrayal
I know the sign is vertical
it brings a moment of true light

we shall plunge into twists and turns of memory
to better understand ourselves
images, rhythms, clarity, illumination
the very organisation of the material universe
Movement and strength engraved in the rocks of the offended earth
Ourselves

and I want to write to wipe away our kisses
and I want to write so not to die
at the feet of the earth where it hurts
This heap of dark dreams
they snuffed out all speech my speech
and my heart which beats faster than lightning
they broke the closed shutters of your look
when dawn grabbed us by the waist

The past is no more than a memory
and midday means I can look at your face
again

tout est à redire tout est à réapprendre
même le langage de l'enfance

Qui osera briser mon chant
dans ce silence atroce
tu es la femme où j'ai mal

J'ai le temps de me taire
l'été va commencer bientôt
et sur le pont du rêve
je veux t'embrasser avec toute ma tendresse

Les oiseaux passent par-dessus nos têtes
et se répondent jusqu'à bercer la mer

Me voici à genoux sur ma terre
face au ciel bleu du midi
dressant mes chants égrenés
à ton ombre illicite

Sinistre est la mémoire
Sinistre est la mort

es-tu devenue one autre mer
un autre ciel sans fond
es-tu devenue un cimetière de cendres.
où le vent éparpille les pierres et les mots

Je sais que tu es mon pays
que tu es le fleuve la source
où mon regard fatigué façonne le temps
et je veux te revoir écriture sur mon corps

Ce soir je suis nu dans ma solitude
Mais voici ma main voici mon coeur
errant à travers le temps
les mots sont les mêmes qu'hier
pour dire l'amour
Le ciel a sa forme de fête

everything must be said again everything relearned
even the language of childhood

Who dares interrupt my song
in this atrocious silence
you are the woman where I hurt

I have time to keep quiet
summer will begin soon
and I want to kiss you tenderly
on the bridge of dreams so tenderly

Birds fly over our heads
respond until they lull the sea

Here I am, on my knees again
facing the blue midday sky
uplifting my scattered songs
to your illicit shadow

Sinister is memory
Sinister is death

have you become another sea
another bottomless sky
have you become a cemetery of ashes
where the wind scatters stone and words

I know that you are my country
that you are the river the source
where my tired eyes fashion time
and I want to see you again like writing on my body

This evening I am naked in my solitude
But here is my hand, here my heart
wandering through time
the words are the same as yesterday
to talk of love
The sky has it own festive shape

et le silence porte l'ombre du passé
je sais que je suis seul
parmi les flots du silence

    * * *

Sachez que je suis un fleuve
je descends par la lave
je descends par les roches
la terre
en silex parmi le jour

Sachez que je suis un fleuve
au bout de ce clair matin d'été
où l'ordre raciste me déclare
rebelle
Mes enfants m'approchent
soleils démultipliés
et noient leurs larmes
dans mon chant

Sachez que je suis le fleuve
la vie la mort
l'instant interminable
et je fixe à jamais l'image de la femme où j'ai mal
dans mon coeur

sans registres d'état civil
qui nous créent et nous régissent
je n'aime pas l'arithmétique
je n'aime pas la haute finance
mais je sais que tu seras mon cri
quand le jour s'émiettera

en milliers de soleils
sur mon corps mêlé à la terre
ma terre
pour que renaissent nos amours

Flora et Georges seront là
Francis et Malcolm seront là eux aussi
Dakeyo de leur seul nom

and silence bears the shadow of the past
I know I am alone
amid the floods of silence

* * *

Bear in mind that I am a river
I flow down through lava
I flow down through rock
earth
flint in the daylight

Bear in mind that I am a river
at the end of this clear summer morning
when the racist order declares me
a rebel
My children come near me
like so many suns
and drown their tears
in my song

Bear in mind that I am the river
life death
the never-ending moment
when I freeze the image of the woman where I hurt
in my heart forever

Without official vital records
that create us and govern us
I do not like arithmetic
I do not like high finance
but I know you will be my cry
when the day crumbles

into thousands of suns
on my body mingled with earth
my earth
for our love to be reborn

Flora and Georges will be there
Francis and Malcolm will be there too
Dakeyo their only name

soleils parmi les soleils
debout portant haut le coeur leur identité

Je songe au départ
et je sais que mon chant envahira
les coteaux fleuris de ma terre
je sais que nous nous mêlerons
à la foule pour fêter le jour final
Et lorsque soufflera la brise matinale
Nous humerons à nouveau le parfum de nos baisers
alors seulement nous tairons nos sanglots
Le jour approche peut-être où je serai
ton homme chargé de promesses

    (unpublished, appeared in Poetry International
    Rotterdam, 1991)

suns among all the suns upright
bearing their identity proudly in their hearts

I dream of the departure
and I know that my song will sweep over
the flowering slopes of my land
I know that we will mingle
with the crowd to celebrate the final day
And when the morning breeze blows
We will once again breathe in the scent of our kisses
only then will we stop sobbing
Perhaps the day is not far off when I will be
your man laden with promise

CHAD

NIMROD

Nimrod Ben Djangrang, known as Nimrod, was born at Koyom, in the south of Chad in 1950. To begin with, he taught French, history, geography and philosophy in Chad and the Ivory Coast. Nimrod says that he writes as a witness of the war that made him flee his home country and to rend homage to his mother, his childhood and the wonder of language itself. Nimrod is a poet, novelist and essayist, and is published notably by Actes Sud and Obsidiane. He received the Louise Labé poetry award for *Passage à l'infini* in 1999 and the Prix Max Jacob 2011 for *Babel, Babylone*.

LE CRI DE L'OISEAU
  à Daniel Bourdanné

J'ai voulu m'enivrer de silence
J'ai délaissé la femme aimée
Je me suis fermé à l'oiseau de l'espoir
Qui m'invitait à gravir les branches
De l'arbre, mon double
J'ai saccagé l'espace de mon jardin
J'ai ouvert mes terroirs
J'ai trouvé agréable l'air qui circule
Entre les vitres. Je me suis réjoui
D'être le sorcier de ma vie
Alors que le soir déroulait ses spectres
L'oiseau en moi de nouveau s'est éveillé
Son cri diffusait l'angoisse
Au sein de mon royaume

TIBESTI (extraits)

  I

Faites, Seigneur, que cette montagne m'épargne,
Et qu'aux ombres du couchant elle s'accroche,
Pénitente. Le ciel, grand ordonnateur, coule sur moi
L'or de la Tripolitaine. Ainsi se concertent un verbe blond,
Une sentence de paille, des beautés transhumantes.
Et quelle lenteur, jardins, pour moi qui veux dormir!
J'ajuste ma faim aux pas des enfants, je traque
Le verbe être, hormis la césure du glaive.
Mes pieds foulent le seuil d'un bref commencement.

  II

Berger, pour toi les étoiles ne somnolent,
Et leur symphonie emplit ton oreille.
Chambrée en ut majeur, elle travaille

THE CRY OF THE BIRD
for Daniel Bourdanné

I wanted to be overcome with silence
I abandoned the woman I love
I closed myself to the bird of hope
That invited me to climb the branches
Of the tree, my double
I created havoc in the space of my garden
I opened up my lands
I found the air that circulates between the panes
Pleasant. I was happy
To be my life's witch doctor
When the evening rolled out its ghosts
The bird in me awoke again
Its cry spread anguish
In the heart of my kingdom

TIBESTI (extracts)

I

O Lord, make this mountain spare me
And cling to the shadows of the setting sun
In penitence. The sky, the great organizer, covers me
With Tripolitanian gold. Thus take counsel, a blonde verb
A straw sentence, transhumant beauty.
Such languor, O gardens, for me who wishes to sleep!
I adjust my hunger to children's footsteps, I hunt down
The verb to be, save for the sword's caesura.
My feet trample the threshold of a brief beginning.

II

Shepherd, for you the stars never sleep,
And their symphony fills your ear.
The tempered piece in C major

Au renouveau du plain-chant. Archivons
Les chemins, la source. Un gazouillis profond
Prononce la paix; une palmeraie y répond.
Et sur nos lèvres l'écho venu de nulle part,
L'obole du rêve. Une montagne survient
Qui, sur l'heure, semble verte.

III

La douceur du matin, ce lieu enfoui et superbe,
Un besoin d'infini. Oasis de Faya-Largeau,
Onguent pour la peau et les yeux, pour la prière
Vous attendrissez nos paupières.
Des paysans régentent les dattiers, leurs fleurs
Ont été fécondées par de justes mains. Les femmes
Auprès de qui nous trouvons asile, dans leur velours
Gras et noir, se destinent à nous avec autorité.

Nous avons gagné le lieu exempt de toute brûlure.
Si nous y taquinons les muses, c'est que la paix
Y remonte des nappes phréatiques.
Le sol fleurit; il orne nos fronts d'une fierté parfaite.

OR L'INFANTE DE SALAMANQUE... (extraits)
(considerations inactuelles sur l'eléphant)

    'L'éléphant est irréfutable.'
                              ALEXANDRE VIALATTE

I

Noli me tangere, telle est sa devise,
Et j'ai gardé la haute main sur la douceur.
Elle anime ses flancs. Cet œil qui me jauge
Est la sûre balance où peser mes pensées.
Ses pieds ont calmé la poussière, apaisé
Ma brûlure. La terre, en sagesse,
Lui ordonne de nous être favorable.

Reworks the plainchant. Let us archive
The paths, the source. A babble deep down
Pronounces the peace: a palm tree replies.
On our lips the echo comes from nowhere,
The offering of the dream. A mountain emerges
That, at the time, looks green.

III

The soft morning, this superb place tucked away,
a need for infinity. Oasis of Faya-Largeau,
balm for skin and eyes, for prayer
You soften our eyelids.
Peasants rule over the date trees, their flowers
were pollinated by just hands. The women
with whom we find asylum, in their thick black
velvet, are destined for us with authority.

We reached this place exempt from any burns.
If we tease the muses here, it is because peace
Rises from the ground water.
The earth blossoms: it adorns our brows with perfect pride.

YET THE INFANTA OF SALAMANCA... (extracts)
(unfashionable considerations on the elephant)

> 'The elephant is irrefutable.'
> ALEXANDRE VIALATTE

I

Noli me tangere, that is his motto,
And I keep supreme control of the softness.
It rouses his flanks. This eye, that sizes me up,
The sound pair of scales to weigh up my thoughts.
His feet calmed the dust, brought relief
To my wound. The earth, wisely,
Orders him to be kind to us.

II

Sa bonté est confiante, sa patience, édifiante.
Pour faire le tour du monde, pour garder le Nord,
Navigateurs, protégez le divin astrolabe
Avec l'exquise étoffe de sa peau.
Vêtement des rois, asile des moines,
Ainsi habillons-nous l'orbe des planètes,
De la Croix-du-Sud à l'étoile du Berger.

III

Son front, sûrement, tient parole. Son teint
Séduit l'asphalte: il y a grand bonheur
À admirer la roche-mère qui nous a vu naître.
Un bonheur odorant, une chanson bien douce.
Qui l'éprouve est bouleversé, qui l'entend
Est pacifié. Ce sont sentiments que les monarques
Voudraient graver sur leur blason.

IV

Prince des ermites, docte animal qui dispense
Son savoir au gré des errances, entre forêt
Et savane, le long des baobabs, au creux des chardons.
La rose de ton œil humide, la science qui l'habite,
Fait reluire la poussière, l'écorce, les épines. Au fronton
Du vieux temple logicien, brille, insigne faveur,
La gloire toujours neuve des grands théologiens.

V

Et quand vient l'heure de la haute retraite,
Quand les princes d'Espagne s'avisent de Salamanque,
Délaissant boucaneries et passions ombrageuses,
Et t'adressent leurs dernières suppliques,
Tu leur conseilles de savoir distance garder.
Et s'ils veulent gagner l'estime des gisants,
Rien ne vaut la gloire des culs-terreux!

II

His kindness is confident, his patience edifying.
To travel round the world, to hold steady North,
Navigators, protect the divine astrolabe
With the exquisite material of his skin.
The cloth of kings, the haven of monks,
Thus do we dress the orbit of planets,
From the Southern Cross to the evening star.

III

His brow, certainly, keeps its word. His colouring
Seduces the asphalt: there is much joy
In admiring the mother-rock that saw us born.
A fragrant joy, a gentle song.
He who feels it is moved, he who hears it
Is calmed. These are sentiments that monarchs
Would like to engrave on their coat-of-arms.

IV

Prince of hermits, learned animal that bestows
Its knowledge throughout its wandering, between forest
And savanna, along baobab trees and through thistles.
The rose within your moist eye, the science therein,
Polishes up the dust, bark and thorns. On the front
Of the old logician temple shines – a signal favour –
The ever-fresh glory of great theologians.

V

And when the time comes to leave worldly things behind, when
The princes of Spain suddenly become aware of Salamanca,
Abandoning their goatish behaviour and sudden passions,
And address you their latest petitions,
You advise them moderation in all things.
And if they want to win the esteem of royal tombs,
There is nothing better than the glory of peasants!

[...]

IX

La douceur, notre cuirasse, on dirait
Qu'elle bat le rappel des nombres entiers.
Parfois, ce sont la terre, le sol, l'écorce du monde
Qui demandent au bel animal d'augmenter
Leur présence d'un front plus haut que le ciel!
La matière vitale est une masse, une momie
Aux organes somptueux, et le sommeil vient
Couronner une marche et dévote et nuptiale.

X

Car le destin de cette peau, le destin mien,
Toile cirée d'un marche-pied si catholique,
N'a pas résisté au dépeçage. Lui reste l'allure,
Métronome des émotions. La douleur,
Cependant, n'a pas réussi à le vaincre.
Chaque jour, l'éléphant s'éloigne,
S'éloigne mon autoportrait...

Pierre, poussière (Obsidiane, 2004)

[...]

IX

The softness, our cuirass, one would say
That it summons up whole numbers.
Sometimes, the earth, the ground, the world's crust
Ask the beautiful animal to increase
Their presence by a brow higher than the sky!
The vital matter is a massive body, a mummy
With sumptuous organs, and sleep comes to
Crown a march that is both pious and nuptial.

X

For the destiny of this skin, my destiny,
The shiny fabric of such a catholic doormat,
Has not resisted dismembering. Only the pace remains,
A metronome of emotions. The pain,
however, has not managed to overcome him.
Every day, the elephant becomes more distant,
And so does my self-portrait...

CONGO BRAZZAVILLE

ALAIN MABANCKOU

ALAIN MABANCKOU was born at Pointe Noire, Congo in 1966. He studied law in Brazzaville and France. His poetry collection *L'usure des lendemains* (Nouvelles du Sud, 1995) was awarded the Prix Jean-Christophe by La Société des Poètes Français. Nostalgia for childhood, love of one's country, the duty to remember, the sense of exile and the decay of contemporary African society are recurring themes treated in lyrical poetry in his collections *La légende de l'errance* (L'Harmattan, 1995), *Les arbres aussi versent des larmes* (L'Harmattan, 1997) and *Quand le coq annoncera l'aube d'un autre jour* (L'Harmattan, 1999). Alain Mabanckou is also a novelist with a focus on Africa, Africans and identity. His fifth novel is called *African Psycho*.

QUAND LE COQ ANNONCERA L'AUBE D'UNE AUTRE JOUR (extraits)

quelque part
l'argile se décompose
dans les profondeurs de la terre

ainsi s'affaisse la roche
et s'entame le cycle
de la géologie préhistorique

un jour l'Histoire s'écrira
sur cet arbre abandonné
les nervures de l'écorce s'entremêleront
le débit de la sève débordera
jusqu'aux racines

et puis mère
comment dire ces mots
tes mots
le parler du pays

la langue d'aujourd'hui
incube des sagaies empoisonnées

dieu nous tourne le dos
la nuit nous plonge dans le tourbillon
la main qui frappe
est celle d'un frère

nous avons en commun
l'ancêtre
le Royaume
et les rites funéraires

WHEN THE COCK ANNOUNCES THE DAWN OF ANOTHER DAY (extracts)

somewhere
clay is decomposing
in the depths of the earth

thus the rock weakens
and the prehistoric
geological cycle starts

one day History will be written
on this abandoned tree
the nervures of the bark will mingle
the coursing sap will brim over
to the roots

and then mother
how does one say these words
your words
country speech

today's language
incubates poisoned assegai

God turns his back on us
night plunges us into the whirlwind
the hand that strikes
is that of a brother

we have in common
the ancestor
the Kingdom
and funeral rites

on pense écrire
et c'est le temps qui force
la main dans son élan
l'ombre qui brouille la vue
le murmure qui obsède l'ouïe
jusqu'à la capitulation
des pensées

il n'y a pas pire
que le deuil des rôniers
le sommeil des marécages
le silence des passereaux

il n'y a pas pire
que les commérages
des fourmis rouges –
les conciliabules des mantes religieuses
les yeux d'agates
dans les antres sombres
le ciel qui se couvre d'un linge plissé

dieu nous tourne le dos

comment lire
la table des lois
traduire les présages
de la nuit
tout était pourtant écrit

l'espace de la durée
se tient sur un fil tenu

les appels lointains
ne sont que les échos
des paroles prisonnières

think of writing
but time forces
the hand into moving
the shadow blurs sight
the whisper pesters hearing
until thoughts
capitulate

there is nothing worse
than the grief of black-rhun palms
the sleep of swamps
the silence of passerines

there is nothing worse
than the gossiping
of red ants
the confabs of praying mantis
eyes of agate
in dark lairs
the sky overcast with folded cloth

God turns his back on us

how can one read
the tables of the law
translate the omens
of night
for everything was already written

the space of a length of time
hangs on a slender wire

far off calls
are only echoes
of captive words

celles d'autrefois
celles raturées dans les grottes

mère
la nuit me couvre depuis
de son immensité

j'ai bâti une hutte
en terre rouge
sur la cime de l'exil
à l'affût des soleils
de ce pays captif de son ombre

ne rien entendre

ils ont blessé les ventricules
de la patrie

la honte se porte sur les visages
comme des masques de fête

qui prononcera le nom de la patrie
à l'aube de la réconciliation

aucune voix ne s'élève par ici
on dit que le silence des plaines
est propice aux assauts

la victoire
est au bout du fusil
disent-ils
vaincre ou mourir
reprennent-ils

those of times past
those erased in grottos

mother
night conceals me since
with its vastness

I have built a hut
with red earth
on the peak of exile
watching out for the suns
of this country captive of its shadow

hear nothing

they wounded the ventricles
of the motherland

their faces covered with shame
like party masks

who will say the name of the motherland
at the dawn of reconciliation

no voice will be raised over here
they say the silence of the plains
is excellent for assaults

victory
is at the end of a gun
they say
conquer or die
they join in

je marche sur la gloire
de leurs faux martyrs
afin de vénérer
de courber la tête
devant le cadavre de cet inconnu

> *Quand le coq annoncera l'aube d'une autre jour* (extraits)
> (Editions L'Harmattan, 1999)

I walk on the glory
of their false martyrs
to venerate
bow my head
before the unknown corpse

TCHICAYA U TAM'SI

TCHICAYA U TAM'SI (1931-1988) was born in Mpili (Congo Brazzaville), but moved to France in 1946 where he died, in Oise, in 1988. Like David Diop, U Tam'si's poetry is colloquial and spoken. Though informal, his work is sophisticated, mocking and rife with dark humour. He juxtaposes vivid historic images and symbolic, even surrealist, renderings of reality, producing a powerful commentary on not only African life, but the human condition. His forays into the meaning of 'black-ness' contribute to Senghor's 'negritude', providing valuable insights into race and significance. A journalist, activist, and strong supporter of Patrice Lumumba, U Tam'si was a vital member of the Congolese independence movement.

AU SOMMAIRE D'UNE PASSION (extraits)

La presse: Édition du matin:
Incident à Léopoldville –
Trois cartes de vœux sur ma
Table exprimant des regrets

Je prête un jeu de cartes aux mains du passant
plus fertiles en dialogues que le destin muet
de mon cœur périssable
qui ne résiste plus au chemin de Damas qu'étreint
le ventre nu d'une colline d'ombre...
Au sommaire de ma passion me dévêtir...

O ma généalogie improbable!
De quel arbre descendre? Quelles fleurs, cet arbre,
fanait-il, avant le glas? Qui sonna le glas?
Un glas comme un pleur d'orpheline dans la nuit!

Un arbre au sommet d'une colline
lève en chandelle une branche de sang :
la branche au poing porte une feuille verte
image d'une flamme à contre-jour jaune et molle,
les djinns la huant!

* * *

Il est des arbres que je ne soupçonne pas
mais d'où me vient cette folie tellement arborescente
que je prends les puces des bois
pour guide dans ma perdition?
De quel arbre descendre?
Je me fais un deuil; de cet arbre improbable.
La nuit est-ce bien mon deuil?....

Je cherchais quand même pillant la forêt vierge,
mes mains pour œillères cherchant
quand un coq éternua à l'orée d'un village
ma voix en berne courba la tête,
un soleil au ciel monta,
un chien sur terre – mystique – absolvait une femme
fit bruit ses mains folles sur ma gorge teinte
de deux lunes froides.

SUMMARY OF A PASSION (extracts)

In the paper: the morning edition:
Incident in Leopoldville –
Three well-wishing cards on
my table expressing sorrow...

I lend a hand of cards to passers by
more fertile in dialogues than the dumb fate
of my perishable heart
that no longer resists the way to Damascus pressed
to the naked belly of a shadowy hill...
To strip at my passion's summary...

O my improbable genealogy!
Descended from what tree? What flowers, shed
from this tree before the knell? Who sounded the knell?
A knell like orphan weeping in the night!

A tree at the hill's summit
lifts its pyrotechnic branch of blood;
the fisted branch carries a green leaf
image of a flame lit against soft yellow,
hallooing of jinns!

* * *

He is of the trees I do not suspect
but from where comes to me this madness so arborescent
I take the wood-lice
for guide in my perdition?
Descended from what tree?
I give up for lost this impossible tree.
Is night truly my loss?...

But all the same I went plundering the virgin forest,
hands groping at blinkers,
when a cock sneezed at the verge of a village
my furled voice bowed its head,
a sun rose into the sky,
on earth – mystical – a dog absolved a woman
made rustle her frantic hands at her bosom colour
of two cold moons.

Le sommeil prit la nuit sous le bras,
il titube sur la plaine et un chien aboie
quand passe le passant disant la bonne aventure
à tout venant, parmi les hibernants... s'ils dorment,
mes frères d'obédience nègre
qui sait de quelle mort je me meurs aimable?

* * *

La presse: Édition du soir –
Des morts et des blessés –
Couvre-feu!

Parmi ce pus de choses bien faites,
pour voir mon meilleur monde,
je me greffe aux rétines deux fleurs d'orangers;
faites qu'elles ne soient de flammes
faites qu'elles soient blanches à refroidir
les morts de ma conscience lente...

Puant cette lenteur, je gagne à triche-cœur
Vienne un meilleur tricheur que moi
me suivant en ce paradis où des hommes
à couteau tiré,
vivent dans leur sommeil
la meilleure part de leur gangrène.
Et celui là,
lèvera-t-il le feu qu'ils éteignent en pillant
le cœur
dont le mystère à peine élucidé
me déshabille m'écorche me crucifie
au sommaire de ma passion?

Extrait de *Épitomé* (P .J Oswald, 1962), republished in *'Arc Musical' précédé de 'Epitomé'*, Introduction de Claire Céa – Préface de Boniface Mongo-Mboussa, Encres Noires, (L'Harmattan, 2007)

Night taken under the wing of sleep,
it totters on the plain and a dog barks
as the wanderer wanders telling all comers
of good luck to come among the hibernating... if they sleep,
my brothers in black obedience
who knows of what death I'm to die adorable?

* * *

In the paper: the evening edition –
Dead and wounded –
Curfew!

To see my better world
among the pus of things well done,
I graft to my retinas two orange-flowers;
grant they be flames
grant they be white enough to chill
the dead of my slow conscience...

Stinking of this sloth, I win by a trick
May a better trickster than I
succeed me in this paradise where men
at knife-point
spend in their sleep
the better part of their gangrene.
And he too,
will he mend the fire they smother plundering
the heart
whose mystery hardly elucidated
strips me scourges crucifies me
at my passion's summary?

DEMOCRATIC REPUBLIC OF CONGO

KAMA SYWOR KAMANDA

KAMA SYWOR KAMANDA was born in Luebo in 1952. Forced to leave the Congo in 1977 due to his political activities, he lived in various European countries before settling in Luxembourg. In 1985, Kama Kamanda founded the Association of African Writers. He draws his inspiration from ancient Egypt and the country of his ancestors and its rich seam of Bantu traditions. Kama Kamanda has received literary accolades such as the Prix Paul Verlaine from the Académie française and the Grand Prix littéraire de l'Afrique noire. His *Œuvres poétiques* (complete works) came out in 2008. The first English language translations of his works – *Tales; Volume One* and a poetry collection called *Wind Whispering Soul* – were published in the USA by Davidson College, North Carolina.

DANS LE SILENCE DES CŒURS

Te voici reine de mon royaume des rêves!
Je me sens, ô femme, perdu en ta profonde nuit
En l'absence de l'étoile du voyageur!
Emporté dans les mouvances de ton âme
Comme dans une mer infinie,
Je me suis noyé dans la lumière de tes désirs:
Ton amour de ses voluptés, m'a transfiguré,
Et j'ai éloigné ma vie des rivages de la solitude.
C'est une douceur dans mon cœur
Nourri du sang des amants!
Les peurs mûrissantes sur les flancs du vent,
Je prie pour que le ciel
Préserve ta vie de toute souffrance,
Et que la force de l'amour sauvegarde ta liberté
Sur toutes les terres où l'honneur
Est une exigence d'élection.
Je traverserai les gouffres de l'amertume
Pour accéder au soleil de ta jouissance,
Et j'atteindrai les plus hauts sommets de tes versants
En mesure que s'en ira en s'élargissant
Le fleuve de toutes les tendresses.

Chants de brumes (Editions L'Harmattan, 1997)

LE CHANT DE LA RÉSISTANCE

Vers les grandes fascinations de la vie,
S'en vont les âmes fanatiques
Sous l'aile protectrice du néant.
C'est aussi l'instant des immenses désillusions
Où se fait sentir la solitude des êtres
Comme une mémoire vidée de messages
Et dépeuplée d'images qui fécondent l'éphémère.
Au-delà du tumulte des guerres,
Un appel au travers des flammes,
Brise les liens qui unissent les hommes à leurs mânes.

IN THE SILENCE OF HEARTS

Now you are queen of my kingdom of dreams!
Woman, I am lost in your darkest night
Without a guiding star!
Carried away by your everchanging soul
As on an infinite sea,
I am drowning in the light of your desires:
Your love of its sensual pleasures transfigured me,
And I distanced my life from the shores of solitude.
It is softness in my heart
Nourished by the blood of lovers!
The fears on the flanks of wind are ripening,
I pray for heaven
To protect your life from all suffering,
And the force of love to safeguard your freedom
Wherever honour
Is a requirement of election.
I will cross gulfs of bitterness
To accede to the sun of your pleasure,
And I will attain the highest summits of your slopes
So that the river of all tenderness will flow down
Broadening as it courses its way.

THE SONG OF RESISTANCE

Fanatical souls advance towards
Life's great fascinations
Under the protective wing of nothingness.
This is also the moment of immense disillusion
When the solitude of being is felt
Like memory voided of its messages
And emptied of images that fuel the fleeting.
Beyond the tumult of war,
A call comes through the flames,
Breaking the bonds that bind men to their manes.

C'est l'heure où les destinées
Se confondent aux étoiles filantes
Et s'épuisent toutes les forces vitales,
Confondant dans le sang et la cendre
Les héros et les martyrs.
Porteurs de laves et de moissons,
Nous irons dans les marais et les forêts, les mers
Et les volcans, apporter les offrandes et les chants.
Nous suivrons les chuchotements des ténèbres
Et les gémissements des ombres
Jusqu'où la racine terrestre s'accouple
Avec les corps célestes
Dans l'écho des mystères lointains.
Nous irons au-delà des Dieux,
Au-delà des chimères, ranimer les esprits
De tous nos morts déracinés.
Nous irons, implacables et dévoués,
Brandissant la foudre comme une étincelle
Dans la nuit de nos souffrances aiguës
Apporter la controverse et les contredits.
Nous irons, sous la pression des vents de l'histoire,
Libérer toutes les consciences
Trop longtemps assujetties.
Les racines de l'arbre à palabres
Finiront par absorber les pluies
En même temps que nos espoirs
Mêlés à l'alchimie des passions.

Le songe des origines (unpublished)

LE CHANT DU DESTIN

Je vais où me guide le vent de l'espérance
Et je poursuis l'astre des existences inachevées.
Le chant du destin accable l'humanité
Des plaintes des croyants.
Ouvrage des morts, prière des disciples,
La rivière s'éloigne avec mes langueurs.
Le maître ivre, le commandeur fou,

This is the hour in which destinies
Become one with shooting stars
And exhaust all life forces,
Mistaking heroes for martyrs
In the blood and ash.
Bearers of lava and harvests,
We will go forward to the swamps and forests, the seas
And volcanoes, to bring offerings and songs.
We will follow the mutterings of darkness
And the groans of shades
Until the earthly root couples
With heavenly bodies
In the echo of distant mysteries.
We will go forward beyond the Gods,
Beyond grotesque visions, to reanimate the spirits
Of all our uprooted dead.
We will go forward, implacable and devoted,
Brandishing lightning like a flare
In the night of our acute suffering
To bring controversy and refutation.
We will go forward, driven by the winds of history,
To free consciences
Subjugated for too long.
The roots of the parley tree
Will end up absorbing the rains
At the same time as our hopes
Mingled with the alchemy of passion.

THE SONG OF DESTINY

I go wherever the wind of hope guides me
I follow the stars of unfinished existences.
The song of destiny overwhelms humanity
With the complaints of believers.
The work of the dead, prayer of disciples,
The river grows distant with my languor.
The master drunk, the commander mad,

Mon illusion absolue d'imiter les Dieux,
T'accorde, ô femme,
Emportée dans l'ivresse des songes
Et le vertige des voluptés,
Un sursis à l'immortalité.
Et la parole sacrée prolonge ta liberté
Où s'enracine la vérité des amours.
Mirage de tous les temps,
Mer d'où s'élancent toutes les passions,
Nature de la beauté,
Ah! Comme dans le soleil de toutes les vies
Et le sang de tous les désirs,
Tu symbolises les miracles des jours!
Ton plaisir vaincu, tes ambitions dénudées,
Et ton ombre abusée, tu trouves ton refuge
Dans l'alchimie des rêves.
Hélas, j'ai caché mes larmes dans la pierre
Lorsque tes yeux se sont ouverts
Dans l'épouvante tragique du déclin des choses.
Les vastes fleuves de la foi
Inondent mon âme débordée et frémissante
Dans le flux et le reflux du songe
Comme une faucille d'or
Au fond des vagues d'une cascade.
Et sur mon corps passent et repassent
Les eaux de l'Histoire.

Les résignations (Editions L'Harmattan, 1997)

MAISONS HANTÉES

Maintenant, nous avons nos doutes pour pleurer.
Quand les identités et les années
Se perdent dans le sable,
Nos villes moroses
Se parfument de roses
Déposées sur les tombes.
Nos maisons hantées
Par de longues solitudes

My absolute illusion of imitating the Gods,
Grant you, woman,
Carried away in the ecstasy of dreams
And dizziness of voluptuous pleasure,
A stay from immortality.
And the sacred word prolongs your freedom
Where the truth of love is rooted.
Mirage of all time,
Sea, from which all passions rise,
The nature of beauty,
Ah! Like the sun of all life
And blood of all desire,
You symbolise the miracle of each day!
Your pleasure vanquished, your ambitions laid bare,
Your shadow abused, you find refuge
In the alchemy of dreams.
Alas, I hid my tears in stone
When your eyes were open
In the tragic terror of the decline of all things.
Vast rivers of faith
Flood my trembling and overflowing soul
In the ebb and flow of the dream
Like a golden sickle
Under a cascade's crashing waves.
And over my body wash back and forth
The waters of History.

HAUNTED HOUSES

Now we have our doubts to cry over.
When identities and years
Become lost in the sands,
Our depressed towns
Smell of roses
Placed on tombstones.
Our houses, haunted
By long periods of solitude

S'ouvrent aux vagues de l'amour,
Aussi abondantes qu'une mer des adieux.
Les offrandes amères
Peuplent les sphères de nos ambitions.
Nous cherchons nos racines
Comme d'autres des vérités cachées.

    Éclipse d'étoiles (Editions L'Harmattan, 1997)

LES ROULEMENTS DU TAMBOUR

Ô toi qui mêles les prières aux souvenirs
Sous les roulements du tambour,
Écoute le chant des femmes et des orphelins
Venus recueillir tes révélations.
Tu murmures les psaumes
Comme des versets du tonnerre
Et tes paroles sont des vents forts
Qui nous déséquilibrent sur le chemin de chimères.
Et toi, symbole de la sagesse millénaire,
Ton sourire de sphinx
Se cache dans la terre de nos luttes.
Te voici maître de nos doutes.
Et comme le soleil de chaque jour,
Tu veilles sur nos pas hésitants
Aux abords du précipice.
Nous te suivrons jusqu'aux confins du rêve
Où nos morts revêtus de lumière
Comme des pagnes translucides
Évitent nos regards audacieux.
Nous nous emparerons de tes légendes
Pour dresser l'esprit des hommes devant les Dieux.

    Le songe des origines (unpublished)

Open up to waves of love,
As abundant as the sea of farewells.
Bitter offerings
People the spheres of our ambitions.
We seek our roots
Like others seek hidden truths.

THE BEATING OF THE DRUMS

O you who mingle prayers with memories
Amid the beating of the drums,
Listen to the songs of women and orphans
Come to gather your revelations.
You murmur psalms
Like verses of thunder
And your words are strong winds
That destabilise us on the path of imaginings.
And you, symbol of the thousand year-old wisdom,
Your sphinx-like smile
Hides in the ground of our struggles.
Here you are master of our doubts.
And like the sun each day,
You watch over our hesitant steps
At the edge of the precipice.
We follow you to the confines of the dream
Where our dead clothed in light
Like translucent pagnes
Avoid our bold looks.
We'll steal your legends
To dress the souls of men before the Gods.

DJIBOUTI

ABDOURAHMAN A. WABERI

ABDOURAHMAN A. WABERI is a writer, novelist and poet. He has won numerous awards, notably the Grand Prix Littéraire de l'Afrique noire in 1996 for his short story collection *Cahier nomade*. In 2000 he published a poetry collection, *Les nomades, mes frères, vont boire à la Grande Ourse* with Editions Pierron, France. An English teacher at Lisieux, in Normandy, Waberi is also an editorial advisor for *Le serpent à plumes* in Paris, and a literary chronicler and writer for *Monde diplomatique*. Recent English translations of his work are the short story collection *The Land without Shadows* (University of Virginia Press, 2005), and the novel *In the United States of Africa (French Voices)* (Bison Books, 2009).

DÉSIRS

je suis le bruissement du monde
le balancement entre ici et ailleurs
la frondaison muette du cactus
le bois rugueux qui recouvre le gecko
le lit du livre-monde
où les pages sont autant de vagues de la quête
toujours recommencée

TRÊVE

je sème ma voix aux quatre coins de la ville
l'eau y dessine le temps
je mêle mon corps aux effluves remontant de la nuit
j'y noie mon désarroi
je cherche dans tes yeux nos querelles d'antan
les clans défaits tissent la toile de leur discorde
je demande aux plantes grasses de me rendre
ma tendre mémoire
      indécise tu écoutes les bruissements de ma brisure
      tu remets à demain
      l'approche de la nuit

ESTAMPES

   1.

entre pierraille et souverain soleil
toute eau bue
toute plainte tue
depuis l'aube
le temps
demeure ce pays:
plaie ouverte sur l'Afrique

DESIRES

I am the rustling of the world
the swaying between here and elsewhere
the dumb foliage of the cactus
the coarse wood that covers the gecko
the bed for the world-book
whose pages are as many waves of the quest
endlessly begun again

TRUCE

I scatter my voice to the four corners of the town
the water shapes time there
I mingle my body with the fragrances that emerge from night
I drown my confusion there
I look into your eyes for our past quarrels
clans undone weaving the web of discord
I ask the succulents to give back
my sweet memory
        indecisive you listen to the rustling of my cracks
        you put off until tomorrow
        the approach of night

ENGRAVINGS

    1.

between scree and sovereign sun
all water drunk
all complaints silenced
since dawn
the time
this country exists:
an open wound on Africa

2.

une géologie torturée
visible à vol d'oiseau
sous chaque pas
une peau desquamée
pas de nuages cendreux
pas encore

3.

fanfaronne
Ardoukoba[1]
depuis qu'il a réveillé les hommes
étaient-ils trop impassibles
à son goût ?

4.

que le Prophète eût à bénir le pays des Habash[2]
– fût-ce en souvenir de Bilal –
n'explique pas l'affliction de ma rive

5.

le troupeau y est plus maigre
        qu'ailleurs
les hommes aussi d'ailleurs

6.

un port
une ville
garnison

---

[1] nom d'un jeune volcan en République de Djibouti
[2] Ethiopie.

2.

tortured geology
visible from a bird's eye view
under each step
flaked skin
no ashen clouds
not yet

3.

braggart
Ardoukoba[1]
since it woke men
were they too impassive
for its liking?

4.

that the Prophet came to bless the country of Habash[2]
– was it in memory of Bilal –
does not explain the affliction of my shore

5.

the herd here is skinnier
         than elsewhere
the men too in fact

6.

port
town
garrison

---

[1] A young volcano in the Republic of Djibouti
[2] Ethiopia.

une simple voie ferrée
un contrefort qu'on disait riche
à l'arrière.

7.

à république miniature
écriture économique

MINIATURES NOMADES
> "There are those who are born of the sun
> Who, by their lips, give life to the withered leaf"[1]
> Mazisi Kunene

1. grand jour

la nuit rêveusement nue
avalées les étoiles
le lance-pierre du jour
attend que le soleil pique son fard
sur la mer inféconde

nous habitons au seuil du soleil
vous ne me croyez pas ?
venez visiter ma maison
si le coeur vous en dit

les couleurs du jour
remontent du puits
   (la nuit)
      la haine verticale se joue du corset tribal

---

[1] "Il y a ceux qui, enfantés par le soleil, / Donnent vie de leurs lèvres à la feuille flétrie" de 'Return of the Golden Age' dans *The Ancestors and the Sacred Mountain*, (Londres, Heinemann, 1982). Mazisi Kunene, poète sud-africain né en 1930, écrit ses textes en zoulou et traduit lui-même en anglais.

one set of tracks
a buttress said to be wealthy
at the rear.

7.

to the miniature republic
an economic entry

NOMADIC MINIATURES

"There are those who are born of the sun
Who, by their lips, give life to the withered leaf"[1]
Mazisi Kunene

   1. the great day

night as in a dream is naked
stars swallowed
the catapult of day
wait for the sun to turn bright red
over the sterile sea

we live on the lintel of the sun
you don't believe me?
come and visit my house
if you're in the mood

   the day's colours
rise up from the well
   (night)
        the vertical hatred scoffs at the tribal corset

---

[1] 'Return of the Golden Age' in *The Ancestors and the Sacred Mountain* (Heinemann, London, 1982). Mazisi Kunene, a South African poet born in 1930, writes his texts in Zulu and translates then into English himself.

    les notes spiralées du muezzin (vacher de l'aube)
viennent de donner le signal aux étoiles moribondes

    2. échos bohèmes pour poème nomade

sur cette terre le poète se meurt
il ne vit que dans le sérail du souvenir
et accumule des menus travaux
des fines aquarelles
des parcelles de vie

une vie encore supportable nous vaut une aimable farce
pas de quoi morigéner une enfance rétive

au lait du jour
je préfère l'encre de la nuit

l'humanité est un maillage
et que dire de ce grand ciel
couleur de terre?

SANS TITRE

je titille le silence sur les grèves de la mémoire
            un ange par dessus mon épaule épie
                  mon cahier suave
                          et

  les mots se cachent dans les plis des pages
           de peur que je ne secoue les draps
             par la fenêtre blanche
              et s'envolent d'un coup d'aile
             les secrets d'alcôve
              ma langue mouillée
                chatouillant le nadir de la feuille
  où se meurt en silence ma semence
            vieille d'un instant

the spiralled notes of the muezzin (the dawn cowherd)
just gave the nod to dying stars

2. bohemian echoes for the nomad poem

on this earth the poet dies
he lives only in the harem of memory
accumulating odd jobs
fine watercolours
scraps of life

life that is still bearable is worth a pleasant joke
not worth taking to task a stubborn childhood

in milky day
I prefer inky night

humanity is a mesh
and what is there to say of this open sky
earth-coloured?

UNTITLED

I titillate silence on the strands of memory
        an angel above my shoulder spies
              my smooth notebook
                      and

  the words hide in the folds of the pages
          afraid that I will shake the sheets
          out of the white window
          and they fly off with a flap of wing
          alcove secrets
          my wet tongue
          tickling the nadir of the sheet
  where my seed, old for an instant,
          dies in silence

LES DITS D'HIER

       Les lèvres féminines de l'orchidée tigrée n'ont
rien à cacher. Nuit noire.
Tout dort, même le silence.
Les os du passé sont là, visibles dans les rues du soir.
Les lauriers pleurent leur Daphnée,
Apollon est parti chasser les jupons en Abyssinie.
Va, jette ton ancre plus loin. Quitte la mer d'Erythrée,
les cieux s'en porteront mieux.
C'est le barde sabre qui vous le dit:
ma terre est maigre, il n'y a rien à vendre.
D'or noir, de bois rare, des perles d'azur?
Rien que du vent, des vents migrateurs –
songes de troupeaux et mirages d'eau.
La confiance en nous s'évapore
comme la rosée du matin
aspirée par l'œil du soleil.
C'est noir, souvent. Rose quelque fois.
Nous sommes loin d'avoir dit oui au rapt du cercueil

    Les Nomades, mes frères vont boire à la Grande Ourse
    (Editions Pierron, 2000)

TALES OF YESTERDAY

      The female lips of the tiger orchid have
nothing to hide. Darkest night.
Everything sleeps, even silence.
The bones of the past here, visible in evening streets.
The laurel trees weep for their Daphne
Apollo is off chasing skirt in Abyssinia.
Go on, anchor further out. Leave the sea of Eritrea,
the heavens will be better then.
This is the sacked bard telling you:
my land is poor, there is nothing for sale.
Black gold, precious wood, pearls of azure?
Nothing but the wind, migratory winds –
the dreams of flocks and mirages of water.
Our confidence has evaporated
like the morning dew
sucked up by the eye of the sun.
It is black, often. Pink sometimes. We are a long way
from having said yes to the abduction of the coffin.

IVORY COAST

TANELLA BONI

TANELLA BONI was born and brought up in Abidjan, Ivory Coast, before going to university in Toulouse and then Paris. She is now a Professor of Philosophy at the University of Abidjan (Cocody). She was the President of the Ivory Coast Writers Association from 1991 to 1997 and is often invited to address international conferences on poetry, the arts and literature. Her most recent poetry collections include *Jusqu'au souvenir de ton visage* (Alfabarre, 2010) and *L'avenir a rendez-vous avec l'aube* (La Roque d'Anthéron, Vents d'ailleurs, 2011). She has also published novels – *Matins de couvre-feu, Les nègres n'iront jamais au paradis* – short stories and children's literature. Tanella Boni has lived in Abidjan for more than twenty years.

LE DON TOUJOURS À VENIR (quatres poèmes)

et il te raconte sa vie la joie
la luisance de sa coquille la béance du son
marin séducteur des mers et des vents

quand il sert ses mots de rire
prince des sables au milieu du repas
même la table redoute que l'humanité prenne fin

à l'orée d'une vie à deux éphémère
cette vie même puits de sens vie bien éphémère
ferme la porte à l'encens d'autres mots sans frontière

    * * *

tout conte dit
l'hominitude n'a rien inventé de neuf sur la terre

chaque parole cheminant vers l'autre
est consolation pour soi seul
quand la barque de l'amour tangue et chavire
au beau milieu de l'infinie solitude de la mer

    * * *

l'homme rêve imagine la rose pour sa femme
l'unique

mais la femme est toujours une autre
marchant à pas divers comme la mer

entre consonne et voyelle
l'amour est toujours une autre histoire

    * * *

et les religions ont fait le tour des idées
dessinés les arbres de la métamorphose du monde

les peaux ne se sont pas rencontrées
les yeux ont eu peur des yeux

THE GIFT STILL TO COME (four poems)

and he recounted his life the joy
the gleam of his shell the gaping sound
sailor seducer of seas and winds

when he uses his words of laughter
prince of sands in the midst of the feast
even the table dreads the end of humanity

at the edge of a fleeting life together
this life even if a well of meaning clearly an ephemeral life
close the door to the incense of other words without frontiers

   * * *

all tales told
hominids have invented nothing new on Earth

each word leading to the next
is consolation for oneself alone
when the boat of love pitches and keels over
in the midst of the infinite solitude of the sea

   * * *

the man dreams imagines the rose for his wife
the only one

but the woman is always another
walking at different paces like the sea

between consonant and vowel
love is always another story

   * * *

and religions have done the rounds of ideas
drawn the trees of the world's metamorphosis

different skins have not met
eyes are afraid of eyes

et les mains ont ignoré le bonjour fraternel
il n'y avait là aucune nécessité

la vie parallèle leur a semblé suivre
le fleuve et le destin de la séparation éternelle

   (previously unpublished)

GORÉE ÎLE BAOBAB (quatre poèmes)

peut-être le bonheur est-il si loin
invisible dans les feuilles de tamarinier
quand ma main effleure les fruits
à partager avec les génies riant des cruautés
faites à l'homme par l'homme

peut-être l'espérance dans mes yeux traîne-t-elle
l'avenir en nuages de poussières où je cherche
étincelles et dignité des âmes en sursis

quand l'horizon au petit matin
dessine images et silhouettes entre soleil et mer
tu n'es pas là pour voir mes yeux
où tu n'a jamais vu l'humeur du monde

   * * *

avec la bénédiction des habitants
invisibles de l'île ici je revis

        car ton regard n'est pas un poème
        mais toute la mer qui coule à mes pieds
        des pages infinies

   * * *

and hands ignored the fraternal greeting
there was no need

this parallel life of theirs appears to follow
the river and destiny of eternal separation

GORÉE BAOBAB ISLAND (four poems)

perhaps happiness is so far away
invisible among the tamarind leaves
when my hand brushes the fruit
to share them with spirits laughing at man's
cruelty to man

perhaps the hope in my eyes drags
the future in clouds of dust where I seek
sparks and the dignity of condemned souls

when the horizon in the early hours
creates images and silhouettes between sun and sea
you are not here to see my eyes
where you have never seen the humour of the world

   * * *

with the blessing of the island's
invisible inhabitants I become alive again

        as your look is not a poem
        but the vast sea that pours infinite pages
           at my feet

   * * *

ici aussi j'ai bu à la source
des mots couverts de moisissures
comme murs suintant de tous les malheurs
gravés aux portes du temps

                j'ai bu la source vive
qui nous donne mémoire et chemin majuscule
            des jours à venir
j'ai bu je ne sais combien de gorgées élixir
              pour la survie du poème
qui hante mes pas depuis toujours

demain je reviendrai
entendre ta voix qui me parle
encore de toi et de moi

    * * *

ici aussi les draps où l'histoire fait la sieste
sont blancs et vides

                    seule la couverture du temps
              est verte comme dernière parole du monde
                    quand le vent tourbillonne
                nuit et jour à la porte du chaos

alors je m'enroule dans les mots de ton regard horizon
par-delà la mer nous séparant infiniment

    Gorée île baobab (Le Bruit des autres / Ecrits des Forges, 2004)

here too I drank at the source
words covered with mildew
like walls oozing all the sorrows
carved on the doors of time

                I drank the life source
that gives us memory and the capped path
              of days to come
I lost count of the mouthfuls of elixir I drank
           so that the poem
that has for ever haunted my steps survives

tomorrow I will return
to hear you talk to me
again of you and me

    * * *

here too the sheets where history snoozed
are white and empty

                        the covers of time alone
              are green like the last word in the world
                      when the wind howls
              day and night at the gates of chaos

then I wrap myself in the words of your look faraway
beyond the sea that separates us infinitely

LEBANON

VENUS KHOURY-GATA

VENUS KHOURY-GHATA is a poet and novelist, resident in France since 1973, author of a dozen collections of poems and as many novels. Her most recent collection, *Où vont les arbres,* was published by Mercure de France in 2011. She was named a Chevalier de la Légion d'Honneur in 2000. Notable awards include the Prix Mallarmé in 1987 for *Monologue du mort.* Her poems have appeared in *Ambit*; *Banipal: a Journal of Modern Arab Literature*; *The Manhattan Review*; *Verse*; and *Jacket* among others. Three collections of Marilyn Hacker's translations of her poetry have appeared: *Here There Was Once a Country* (Oberlin College Press, 2001) and *She Says* and *Nettles* (Graywolf Press, 2003 and 2008, respectively).

LES OBSCURCIS (extraits)
pour Claude Estéban

1.

Nous nous sommes exclus de l'espace informe de l'air
pour une terre soucieuse de combler ses excavations avec os
                                        chiffons aboiements
nous avons perdu cette mobilité qui faisait de nous
des objets reconnaissables à leur contour
viables entre azote et asphalte
nous nous sommes décolorés

2.

Egaux lors de la distribution des tâches
      et pour éviter toute revendication
on nous serra en fagots silencieux
sans préciser à quelle forêt nous appartenions
sans accès à nos noms placés plus haut que nous
lisibles des murs debout sur leur unique pied

3.

Les rumeurs de la ville nous arrivent disloquées
les reconstituer en ligne droite exige le savoir faire
d'un arpenteur du cadastre

les voix chevauchant les pierres
l'écho chevauchant les voix
s'allongent jusqu'aux maisons renversées
drap ou linceul qu'importe

4.

Donnez-moi une boite d'allumettes où me réfugier
deux pétales de rose pour me nourrir
et que le monde soit gouverné par une cigale

THE SHADES (extracts)
for Claude Estéban

1.

We excluded ourselves from the formless space of air
for an earth anxious to fill in its excavations with bones,
                                                                     rags, barking
we lost this mobility that makes us
objects recognizable by their contour
viable between nitrogen and asphalt
we become washed out

2.

Equals, during the handing out of tasks
       to avoid any protest
we were bunched into silent bundles of firewood
without being told exactly to which forest we once belonged
without access to our names placed higher up than us
legible from walls upright on their one and only base

3.

The clamour of the town reaches us all broken up
piecing it together into a straight line requires
the skill of a surveyor

voices overlapping the stones
echo overlapping voices
lying stretched out until the upturned houses
sheet shroud whatever

4.

Give me a matchbox I can take refuge in
two rose petals so I can eat
and may the world be governed by a cicada

Nous glissons
glissons avec la planète
nous maigrissons pour nourrir des cloisons faméliques de
                                                                    notre chair
Personne n'a le bras assez long pour ouvrir à l'air souterrain
personne n'a l'énergie nécessaire pour préparer la mue
de trépas à vie
Personne n'a localisé le passage prohibé

    5.

Nous limons nos aspérités pour ne pas éveiller la méfiance de
ceux qui nous prennent pour des loups
pour des instruments émettant le même son osseux
Certains nous assimilent à des caisses de clameurs maniées par
                                                                                    le vide
alors que nous pataugeons sans cesse dans nos étuis
n'accusant personne de la restriction de nos déplacements en
                                                                   dehors de nous
Drap ou linceul qu'importe

    6.

Les nostalgiques cherchent leur forme dans leurs vêtements évaporés
ignorant que le chagrin ne retient pas le lin
et que des jardiniers vigilants plient dans le même sens chair et écorce
Les rêveurs attendent la saison des lucioles pour copuler
les millions de battements d'ailes limant les aspérités
le rien pénètre le rien
nous nous emboîtons
feignons des coïts
que les austères s'enterrent de leurs propres mains
alors qu'ils le sont déjà
et qu'il n'y a pas plus mort qu'eux
drap ou linceul qu'importe

    […]

We glide along
glide along with the planet
we lose weight to feed the scraggy septums of our flesh
Nobody has arms long enough to open the underground
                                              passage to the air
Nobody has the energy needed to prepare for the changing
from the next world to this
Nobody has found the forbidden passage

   5.

We file off our harshness so not to awaken the mistrust
of those who take us for wolves
for instruments that emit the same bony sound
Some liken us to crates of strident noise tossed by emptiness
while we flounder about ceaselessly in our cases
accusing nobody of curbing our movement outside our selves
Sheet shroud whatever

   6.

Those who hark back seek their shape in their vanished clothes
unaware that sorrow does not retain the linen
and that vigilant gardeners fold both flesh and bark along the
same lines
Dreamers wait for the firefly season to copulate
the millions of beating wings filing the bumps
void penetrates void
we fit closely together
feigning coitus
that austere people bury with their own hands
whilst they are already buried
and nothing could be more dead than they
Sheet shroud whatever

   […]

C'était courant à l'époque d'accompagner le jour jusqu'au
cimetière
avec le soleil qui s'effritait de désolation pour les lucioles qui le
relayaient
nous cherchions les prairies à la lueur des lanternes
criions leur nom jusqu'au ravin
puis les ramenions par la peau du cou dans l'étable
les brebis de l'année dormaient
dans les arbres tout était palpable même l'écho
et le sentier traversé se roulait tel tapis d'orient
en prévision de l'hiver
nous escaladions la montagne
comme une nature morte

    Unpublished version of a poem later published in *Les Obscurcis* (Mercure de France, 2008)

It was usual back then to accompany day to the cemetery
with the sun falling apart with grief for the fireflies that came next
we searched meadows by lantern light
crying out their name until the ravine
then dragging them back by the scruff to the stable
the year's flock slept
in the trees everything was palpable even the echo
the path travelled rolled out like an oriental carpet
in anticipation of winter
we scaled the mountain
like a still life

MAURITIUS

EDOUARD MAUNICK

EDOUARD MAUNICK was born in Mauritius in 1931. He has been, successively, author and producer of radio programmes, TV presenter, editor of *Jeune Afrique*, a director at UNESCO and Mauritian Ambassador to Pretoria. Since 1954, he has published more than twenty collections of poetry, the most recent of which is *50 quatrains pour narguer la mort* (Quatre Bornes, Mauritius & Seghers, Paris). Edouard Maunick has been awarded the Prix Apollinaire, and is a member of the Haut conseil de la Francophonie and a Chevalier des Arts et Lettres.

J'ÉTAIS UN ARBRE AUTREFOIS

   1.

... si jamais le jour se lève
sans n'avoir rien cédé
des manèges de la lumière
ce qui ne donne pas à voir
jusqu'à l'âme déguenillée
un corps déjà malhabile
à porter le poids des ans

   2.

...si jamais la nuit s'annonce
sans n'avoir rien payé
de la dette de paquets de rêves
où le poème avalise
le voyage de longs sommeils
à toujours revisiter
mêmes contrées de déshérence

   3.

...alors paroles imitent nues
rumeurs poussière de silence
descendue sur le grand âge
en saison crépusculaire
certes tout n'est pas accompli
mais combien mauvais le signe
quand l'arbre totem ne saigne plus

   4.

...quel vide sans le végétal
sans racine inaugurale
l'aube souterraine de l'ébène
de la fougère et de l'herbe
humides du sang de le terre

I ONCE WAS A TREE

   1.

...if ever day rises
having ceded nothing
of merry-go-rounds of light
that does not allow even
the ragged soul to see
a body already awkwardly
bearing the weight of years

   2.

...if ever night nears
having paid back none
of the debt dreams amassed
where the poem guarantees
a journey full of deep sleep
forever revisiting
the same escheated lands

   3.

...then speech imitates naked
rumours dust of silence
descended on old age
in the crepuscular season
true all is not accomplished
but terrible is the sign
the totem tree no longer bleeds

   4.

...what a void with no plant life
without inaugural root
underground dawn of ebony
fern or grass
damp with earth blood

tout cela qui perce et pousse
pour donner un visage au monde

    5.

...tout cela que je raconte
avec des mots cabossés
la juste et l'injuste folie
d'avoir longtemps regardé
la mer et de m'être laissé prendre
au jeu de l'interroger
sur l'horizon immobile

    6.

...qu'y a-t-il de si sorcier
de l'autre côté des brisants
sinon une ligne au lointain
oublieuse de cadencer
ce qui l'aurait métissée
avec le reste de la danse
secrète des grands fonds marins

    7.

...voilà bien des années que
nous croyons savoir relire
l'évangile des océans
ses versets et ses proverbes
baptiser de noms étranges
les lieux où la mer s'épelle
en lettres douces et barbares

    8.

...sonnent et résonnent au hasard
Gorée triste embarcadère
d'une nègre cargaison
alors que bandonéonne

all that pierces and grows
to give the world a face

    5.

...everything I recount
with battered words
the just and unjust folly
of long contemplating
the sea, of being taken in
by the game of questioning
the motionless horizon

    6.

...what is so magic
the other side of the breakers
save a far off line
knowingly forgetful to rhythm
what would've crossed it
with the rest of the secret
dance of the deep seabed

    7.

...so it's been years since
we thought we could reread
the gospel of oceans
its verses and proverbs
to baptise with strange names
places the sea spells
in soft and savage letters

    8.

...tolls and randomly resounds
Gorée sad landing stage
for Negro cargoes
as bandoneons sound

Buenos Aires coeur tango
d'égale nègre palpitation
sans vouloir hâler le monde

    9.

...à réciter rades et ports
à toutes les heures des cités
l'Histoire avalise l'histoire
à hauteur de mille légendes
de Salaline l'insulaire
à Mumbai en Mer d'Oman
où rit et pleure un enfant

    10.

...je brûle d'évoquer les îles
Haïti béante blessure
que le Poème cautérise
Robben Island et Cuba
entre séquestre et liberté
et ma terre clamée plurielle
mais de singulière alarme

   [previously unpublished]

Buenos Aires heart of tango
equal to negro pulsating
without so embrowning the world

   9.

...to tell of harbours and ports
all cities at all hours
History endorses history
equal to a thousand legends
from insular Salamine
to Mumbai in the Arabian Sea
where a child laughs or cries

   10.

...I long to talk of the islands
Haiti the burning wound
that the Poem cauterises
Robben Island and Cuba
between isolation and freedom
my land proclaimed plural
but of singular alarm

KHAL TORABULLY

KHAL TORABULLY was born in 1956. He has a doctorate in poetic semiology and his collections include *Palabres à parole* (1997), *L'ombrage rouge des gazelles* (1998) and *Chair corail, fragments coolies* (Editions Ibis Rouge, Guadeloupe, 1999), which won the 2000 Prix du Livre Insulaire. Co-editor of the review *Missives*, Torabully is also writer-director of four films, including *La Mémoire Maritime des Arabes* (Chamarel Films, with the backing of the Sultanate of Oman; English and Arabic versions, TV Oman). He has also published *Kot sa parol la? Rôde parole* (bilingual, Creole / French, 1995) and most recently *Cahier d'un retour impossible au pays natal* (Editions K'A, Ille-sur-Têt, 2009).

CANTATE POUR L'ENFANT DE CANA (extrait)

Enfant au visage suspendu entre le crépuscule
Des pieux et l'aube des mots,
Ton silence est ouverture qui module
Déploration et tombeau.
Il est dictée musicale
Et frisson des peaux.

Ton cri, tu sais le réorchestrer,
Le contrepointer,
L'arpéger,
Le fuguer,
Le bémoliser,
Le syncoper,
Le diéser,
Le moduler,
Le rythmer.

Le cri de l'enfant est la plus belle résistance,
Avant qu'un écrit ne brise le silence!

Cantate pour l'enfant de Cana (unpublished)

LES INDIADES, ODES À PASSOA (extrait)

Saudade en cassant mes syllabes:
J'ai traversé archives et archipels
Dans l'encolure des ancolies.
Fougueux comme le fauve menacé
Je fuis l'ombre comme le marron des pénombres.

CANTATA FOR THE CHILD FROM CANA (extract)

Child, face suspended between twilight
of the pious and dawn of words,
your silence an overture that modulates
lamentation and tomb.
Musical dictation
and shivering skin.

You are able to re-orchestrate,
counterpoint,
arpeggiate,
fugue,
flat,
syncopate,
sharpen,
modulate,
rhythm your cry.

The child's cry the best form of resistance,
until a text breaks the silence!

THE INDIADES, ODES TO PESSOA (extract)

Saudade[1] by breaking my syllables:
I crossed archives and archipelagos
In the collum of columbine.
Fiery as the threatened big cat
I flee the shade like the marron of penumbra.

---

[1] *Saudade* is a Galician / Portuguese word for a feeling of nostalgic longing for something or someone that one was fond of, now lost and probably never to return.

Saudade:
Ton geste de femme
Est clapotis d'eau aux ravines des rosées.
Au sud la légende fragile
Brise l'alliance de l'aube et l'aubépine.

Saudade:
En unités de soleil mesurer les salines.
Découpé dans le miroir, ton rêve,
Brisé dans la clarté de ton cri.

Saudade:
Ta respiration croit dans les mots perdus.
Ta parole est le nuage noir que déplace le cyclone.
Coupée dans le cristal, ta lumière aphone.

Saudade:
Pour que le soleil s'obstine à peser ta bouche.

   Les Indiades, Odes à Pessoa (unpublished)

LUMIÈRE SOMBRE SUR L'AAPRAVASI GHAT (extraits)

Je lave tes pieds
DANS CE PAYS CALCINÉ
PAR LE LENT SOLEIL
Une telle concession faite aux oublis
Face à ce continent brûlé par le mépris

POIDS DE NOVEMBRE
REPRESSION DE septembre
J'ai ponctué les mois de fruits amers
Et les mois de lunes froissées

Par la défaite de nos rémissions
Par la détresse de premières dénonciations
Revient la sécheresse des cœurs friables,

Saudade:
Your womanly gesture
Is lapping water in ravines of dew.
To the south the fragile legend
breaks the union of dawn and hawthorn.

Saudade:
Units of sun to measure salt marshes.
Jagged in the mirror, your dream
Broken in the clarity of your cry.

Saudade:
Your breathing grows stronger in lost words.
Your words are the black cloud displaced by the hurricane.
Crystal cut, your voiceless light.

Saudade:
So the sun stubbornly still weighs your mouth.

DARK LIGHT CAST ON AAPRAVASI GHAT (extracts)

I wash your feet
IN THIS COUNTRY SCORCHED
BY THE SLOW BURNING SUN
such a concession to what is forgotten
faced with this continent burnt by scorn

THE WEIGHT OF NOVEMBER
REPRESSION OF September
I punctuated the months of bitter fruit
and months of crumpled moons

with the defeat of our forgiveness
with the distress of the first denunciations
thus returns the drought of friable hearts,

Le vertige du lézard dans le labyrinthe des feuilles.
Ta bouche repue des couleurs du gecko
Imite la première errance des chats.

   [...]

Mes pieds nus cherchent l'impossible lieu
de mon nadir. J'enlève l'ocre habit de terre,
soleil collé au front viscéral de ma tâche.

Île mienne, il faut mettre
la terre en prémonition,
et retracer les contours
de la carte bleue du voyage.
Là-bas,
l'Inde et le soleil dominent les yeux rouges
des araignées.

Terre natale accrochée au fil
de mes rêves tissés et retissés,
réticents ?

   Lumière sombre sur l'Aapravashi Ghat (unpublished)

CALE D'ÉTOILES, COOLITUDE (extraits)

Coolitude pour poser la première pierre de ma mémoire de toute mémoire, ma langue de toutes les langues, ma part d'inconnu que de nombreux corps et de nombreuses histoires ont souvent déposée dans mes gènes et mes îles.

À me demander si je fais partie d'une race de malaxeurs d'épices et de parfums, de soies et d'ors, de pigments de peaux et de mots.

Coolitude, mon roulis-coolie, chant d'un enracinement autant que chant d'un déracinement dans une terre faite d'autres poussières, rencontre nécessaire où l'indien apporte son cuivre millénaire au chant du monde.

lizard giddy in the labyrinth of leaves.
your mouth gorges on the colours of the gecko
imitates the first wanderings of cats.

[...]

My bare feet seek the impossible place
of my nadir. I remove the ochre garment of earth,
sun glued to the visceral forehead of my task.

My island, we have to put
the earth in a state of foreboding
retrace the contours
of the blue travel map.
Over there,
India and the sun overwhelm the red eyes
of spiders.

Birth country suspended to the thread
of my woven rewoven dreams,
reluctant perhaps?

HOLD FULL OF STARS, COOLITUDE (extracts)

Coolitude lay the first stone of my memory of all memory,
my tongue of all tongues, my share of the unknown that
many bodies many stories have often laid down
in my genes and my islands.

Wondering if I belong to a race of kneaders of spices and
perfumes, of silks and gold, of skin pigments and words.

Coolitude, my ruley-coolie, song of rootedness as much
song of uprootedness in an earth made of other specks of dust,
necessary meeting where the Indian brings his millennial copper
to the song of the world.

Pour dire nos voyages, nos rencontres et nos métissages
incessants ; voici mon chant d'exil et de bonheur: avant d'être homme
nouveau, je suis homme en devenir.

   [...]

Coolitude non seulement pour la mémoire... mais aussi pour ces
valeurs d'hommes que l'île a échafaudées à la rencontre des fils
d'Afrique de l'Inde de Chine et de l'Occident.
Pour moi, la seule patrie rêvée est celle de la grande
fraternité... de la réconciliation.

Coolitude: parce que je suis créole de mon cordage, indien de
mon mât, européen de la vergue, je suis mauricien de ma quête et
français de mon exil. Je ne serai toujours ailleurs qu'en moi-même
parce que je ne peux qu'imaginer ma terre natale...

Est-ce pour cela que ma vraie langue maternelle est la poésie ?

   Cale d'étoiles, Coolitude (Azalées Éditions, La Réunion, 1992)

DIALOGUE DE L'EAU ET DU SEL (extraits)

Le dialogue n'est pas plus lieu qu'espace,
ni cri où l'être naît et trépasse.

Il est soudaine traversée, suite d'épitaphes
où l'âme sème trace au silence calligraphe.

Pourtant, entre le ciel et l'eau, seul le mot
rend l'être inquiet: entre corail et rocaille,
l'instant de parole – ce roseau qui s'emplit enfin d'une note
qui tressaille.

Que le grain de sel et l'eau défassent la mer
ou le silence, là n'est pas mon affaire.
Mais qu'enfin ici se nomme la Frontière,

To tell you of our incessant travels, our meetings, our cultural mixing;
here is my song of exile and happiness: before I become a new man,
I am a budding man.

[...]

Coolitude not only for memory... but also for these
values of mankind the isle amassed for the meeting of sons
from Africa, India, China and the West.
For me, the only fatherland dreamed is that of the great
brotherhood... of reconciliation.

Coolitude: because I am Creole through my rigging, Indian
by my mast, European by the yard, Mauritian through quest and
French through exile. I will only be elsewhere in myself
because my native land exists only as I imagine...

Is that why poetry is my real mother tongue?

DIALOGUE OF WATER AND SALT (extracts)

Dialogue is no more a place than space,
nor cry where being is born and trespasses.

It is a sudden crossing, a succession of epitaphs
where the soul leaves traces in the calligrapher's silence.

Yet, between sky and water, the word alone
disquiets the being: between coral and rock,
the instant of speech – this reed finally full of notes
that quiver.

If salt and water wish to undo the sea
or silence, that's not my business.
But if this here is the Frontier,

entre désir et dire, je l'inscris en pleine chair.
La mer est plus loin que le sel
le sel plus près que la mer.

> [...]

Parle! Parle! Dis-moi le dialogue de l'eau!
Parle! Parle! Dis-moi les arabesques du sel!
Au sens inverse des mots,
Parle ma mémoire, avant que je ne t'ascende!

Dialogue de l'eau et du sel (Les Bruits des Autres, 1998)

L'OMBRE ROUGE DES GAZELLES (extrait)

Je n'avais jamais vu Guernica au centre de mon marché.
Les fruits éventrés par des lames damnables,
les légumes creusés aux griffes des bitumes.
Cette tête figée en sanglots,
Cette mère déchirée de sa vie,
cet enfant coupé à la gorge de son rire.

Le croissant rouge flotte dans un ciel livide,
mes yeux s'égarent à la première explosion des astres:
le thé s'est renversé dans un vol d'oiseaux effarouchés.

Je n'avais jamais vu l'horreur dépecée aux yeux du jour,
tant d'ombres méconnaissables dans les débris du monde effaré.
Les fous, quels fous peuvent se réclamer d'une folie bénie?
Les fous, quelle raison plus grande que le rêve décapité?
Les têtes à l'envers,
ma terre divague,
le ciel à corps perdu,
j'hallucine du nord au sud.

L'ombre rouge des gazelles, signes pour Algérie, (Paroles d'Aube, 1998)

between desire and speech, I note it in flesh and bone.
The sea is further out than salt
salt closer than sea.

[...]

Speak! Speak! Tell me the dialogue of water!
Speak! Speak! Tell me the arabesques of salt!
The opposite meaning of words,
Speak memory, before I take you out!

THE RED SHADOW OF GAZELLES (extract)

I had never seen Guernica in the middle of my market.
Fruit disembowelled by damnable blades,
vegetables furrowed by the claws of asphalt.
This rigid head in tears,
This mother torn from her life,
this child throat cut in mid-laugh.

The red crescent floats in a livid sky,
my eyes stray at the first explosion of stars:
tea spilt in a flight of alarmed birds.

I had never seen horror dismembered before the eyes of day,
so many unrecognisable shades in the debris of the aghast world.
Madmen, which madmen can call on sacred insanity?
Madmen, what greater reason than the headless dream?
Heads upside down,
my earth raving,
heaven headlong,
I hallucinate north to south.

MOROCCO

ABDELLATIF LAÂBI

ABDELLATIF LAÂBI was born in Fès in 1942. He published his first poetry collection at the age of 20. With fellow Moroccans, he founded the journal *Souffles* in early 1966 and the publishing house Atlantes. He also founded, along with Moroccan dissident Abraham Sefaty, the Association de Recherche Culturelle (ARC). This body was swiftly targeted by the government, and both men were arrested. Laâbi was imprisoned for various reasons, and on numerous occasions, in the 1970s. He was not freed until 18 July 1980, apparently on account of pressure from European intellectuals and because of the numerous awards he had won. He moved to France in the 1980s, where he became a permanent resident in 1995. His latest poetry collection, *Œuvre poétique II*, was published by Editions La Différence, Paris, in 2010.

TABLE RASE
PETITE (extraits)

Juste un corps
avec une tête
et ce qui s'ensuit
pour sonder
le vertige de l'infini
l'étendue du mal
les tempêtes contrariées
de l'amour
Les questions idiotes
se présentent en premier
chassées séance tenante
dans un sursaut de fierté
Ordre du jour
rien de moins que
la table rase

  […]

D'une main
rouler distraitement
la pâte sans levain
du désir
De l'autre
la plus ferme
dessiner la courbe du temps
en se mordant la langue
Et que les yeux restent rivés
sur le feu
déclaré au préalable

  […]

Le mot
oiseau déplumé
échoué sur ton parchemin
au lieu de le caresser
tu l'ingères
en étouffant les bruits de déglutition
et tu guettes le suivant

SMALL CLEAN SLATE (extracts)

Just a body
with head
and what follows
to probe
the spiral of infinity
the extent of evil
the thwarted storms
of love
Idiotic questions
first spring to mind
chased away forthwith
in a burst of pride
Agenda:
nothing less
than a clean slate

    [...]

One hand
absently kneads
the unleavened dough
of desire
The other
firmer
traces the curve of time
biting its tongue
And eyes remain riveted
to the flame
avowed beforehand

    [...]

The word
a plucked bird
stranded on your sheet
you refrain from stroking
you ingest it
stifling the swallowing sound
and watch for the next

qu'une fourmi langagière
poussera imprudemment
jusqu'à le faire tomber
dans ton escarcelle
Le lecteur cannibale
a de qui tenir

LES ÉPAULES ET LE FARDEAU (extraits)

Elle est bien belle
l'Afrique d'aujourd'hui!
C'était hier
– et c'est déjà irréel –
que nous avons célébré les noces
de sa liberté retrouvée
et l'épousée
encore plus désirable que dans nos rêves
"vêtue de sa couleur qui est vie"
insolemment jeune
exhibant sa fleur et ses seins d'ardeur
conduisant la transe
qui rend l'âme au corps
la lumière aux yeux
la parole inspirée à la bouche
Sa négraille enfin debout
unie dans la reconnaissance du sang
seule couleur agréée de l'homme
C'était hier
jour orphelin
d'une genèse avortée

   [...]

Africa!
Tes peuples parias
rameaux rabougris de la souche originelle
conçue dans ton limon
Tes peuples errants
dans la fournaise glacée d'un enclos

that a linguistic ant
will unwisely nudge
until it falls
into your net
The cannibal reader
has the grist it needs

SHOULDERS AND THE BURDEN (extracts)

Today's Africa
is truly beautiful!
It was only yesterday
– which already seems unreal –
that we celebrated the wedding
of its regained freedom
and married it
even more desirable than we dreamed
"dressed in the colour of life"
insolently young
flaunting flower and breasts of fervour
leading the trance
that gives soul back to body
light to eyes
inspired words to mouth
Its negritude finally upright
united in the recognition of blood
the only agreed colour of man
Yesterday
the orphan day
of an aborted origin

    […]

Africa!
your pariah peoples
stunted branches of the original root
conceived in your silt
Your wandering peoples
in the frozen furnace of a pen

à la dimension du Continent
Tes peuples aveuglés
attelés
ployant sous le joug
faisant tourner la meule
qui écrase
les fruits de leurs entrailles
Les envieux
qui vantaient insidieusement ta jeunesse
t'ont condamnée à mourir jeune
L'extinction annoncée de l'espèce
commencera par toi

    [...]

La connaissance ne pardonne pas
Elle te ronge
De quoi serais-tu coupable?
D'un quelconque oubli
ou de surenchère
De te sentir brûler avec les mots
que tu as mis sur l'innommable
et de rester vissé sur ton siège
en sirotant ton café?
Ose le dire:
même innocent du mal
tu en es l'otage
Peut-on pacifier le cœur des bourreaux
changer d'humanité?
Personne n'a la réponse
La rédemption, la Rédemption
murmures-tu
cette équation insoluble

    [...]

Ce n'est pas une affaire d'épaules
ni de biceps
que le fardeau du monde
Ceux qui viennent à le porter
sont souvent les plus frêles
Eux aussi sont sujets à la peur
au doute

the scale of the Continent
Your blinded peoples
harnessed
ploughing under the yoke
turning the millstone
that crushes
the fruit of their womb
Those envious people
that insidiously praised your youth
condemned you to die young
The heralded extinction of the species
will start with you

   [...]

Knowledge does not forgive
It eats away at you
What would you be guilty of?
Of some oversight or other
or overstatement
To feel yourself burning with the words
you gave the unspeakable
but remain glued to your chair
while sipping a coffee?
Dare to say it:
even if innocent of evil
you are hostage to it
Can one give peace to torturers' hearts,
change humanity?
Nobody has the answer
redemption, Redemption
you murmur
this unsolvable equation

   [...]

It is not a matter of shoulders
or biceps
only the world's burden
Those who are able to bear it
are often the frailest
They too are prone to fear
doubt

au découragement
et en arrivent parfois à maudire
l'Idée ou le Rêve splendides
qui les ont exposés
au feu de la géhenne
Mais s'ils plient
ils ne rompent pas
et quand par malheur fréquent
on les coupe et mutile
ces roseaux humains
savent que leurs corps lardés
par la traîtrise
deviendront autant de flûtes
que des bergers de l'éveil emboucheront
pour capter
et convoyer jusqu'aux étoiles
la symphonie de la résistance

    All poems from *Tribulations d'un rêveur attitré* (Editions de La Différence, 2008)

despondency
and sometimes driven to curse
the splendid Idea or Dream
that exposed them
to the fire of Gehenna
But while they may bend
they do not break
and when by frequent misfortune
they are slashed and mutilated
these human reeds
know that their bodies hacked
by treachery
will become as many flutes
that shepherds at daybreak
raise to their lips
to capture
and convey to the stars
the symphony of resistance

SENEGAL

BABACAR SALL

BABACAR SALL is Maître de conférences at the University of Cheikh Anta Diop in Dakar, where he carries out research in Egyptology and on ancient Africa in general. He collaborated on the UNESCO's *History of Humanity: Vol. II – From the Third Millennium to the Seventh Century B.C.*, a period that encompasses the transition from prehistory to history with the advent of writing. He has notably written for *ANKH*, a journal of Egyptology and African Civilisations. His publications include *Racines éthiopiennes de l'Egypte ancienne* (L'Harmattan, 1999); *Les voix de l'aube* (L'Harmattan, Poètes de cinq continents); and *Le lit de sable: Poème* (L'Harmattan, Poètes de cinq continents). He is also assistant editor at Editions l'Harmattan.

LE LIT DE SABLE (extraits)

Ma tête ne vaut même pas
Le grain de sable
Qui survit à l'homme
Au ver de terre prédateur
De ma chair solide et liquide
Comme un citron vert

Le sommeil imite la mort
Jusqu'à la démence
Et finit par corrompre
L'élan vital de l'éveil
Au matin de l'homme
Quand un ange furtif
Vient aspirer en catastrophe
Les dernières poches d'air de l'être
Qui s'affaissent comme des pneus crevés

J'ai construit une tour de verre
Haute comme mille hommes juxtaposés
Dont les crânes rasés servent de marches
À mes escaliers bien cirés
Que je n'emprunte que pour contempler
La bassesse de mes courtisans
Qui confondent grandeur
Et hauteur de demeure

Je me croyais invincible
Jusqu'au jour où d'infimes créatures
Envahirent mon corps
Et creusèrent des galeries souterraines
Dans mes veines obstruées
Vidant mon sang corrompu
Mon flot d'eau usée

BED OF SAND (extracts)

My head is not even worth
the grain of sand
that survives man
and worm predator
of my flesh, solid, liquid
like a lime

Sleep imitates death
until dementia
ends up corrupting
the vital sap of stirring
at the dawn of man
when a furtive angel
urgently inhales
the last air pockets for the being
that sags like a slit tyre

I built a glass tower
high as a thousand apposed men
whose shaven heads were steps
for my highly polished stairs
I only use to contemplate
the grovelling of my courtesans
who confuse grandeur
with the size of a house

I thought I was invincible
until the day tiny creatures
invaded my body
and dug underground galleries
in my obstructed veins
emptying my corrupted blood
my spate of wastewater

Affaibli par la douleur
Et crachant mes remords
Je m'étonne que de telles moisissures
Puissent nuire à tant de grandeur

Mon corps rongé par ces maux
Flétrit en tige de mil asséchée
J'ordonne qu'on me descende du lit
Pour m'allonger par terre
Mais le plancher marbré
Fait craquer mes os
Ossature de branches mortes

Je demande qu'on me retire
De ma tour de verre
Pour que l'oxygène irrigue mes poumons
Et y dépose son parfum frais
Mais tout me suffoque
Même l'air dont l'haleine
Pue comme un péché

J'exhorte qu'on me débarrasse
De mes accessoires encombrants
Pour que tout nu
Je montre au monde admiratif
Mes blessures ouvertes
Avant que la terre brûlante
Ne me dévore dans ses entrailles

Me voila nu dans ma savane
Qui m'a vu naître nu
En grains de sable
Qui choient au moindre fracas
Je compte sur l'enfant
Qui m'aidera à me relever
Pour rendre à la terre son fertilisant
Son fruit illusoire de minuit

Weakened by pain
coughing up my remorse
I am astonished such mildew
could tarnish so much grandeur

My body gnawed by ills
withers to a dried millet stalk
I tell them to lift me out of bed
lay me on the ground
but the marbled floor
cracks my bones
this skeletal dead-branch frame

I ask them to remove me
from my glass tower
so oxygen can irrigate my lungs
and leave behind its spark
but everything smothers me
even the air whose breath
stinks like sin

I urge them to get rid
of my burdensome accessories
so that stark naked
I can show an admiring world
my open wounds
before the burning earth
devours me in its entrails

Here I am naked in my savannah
which saw me born naked
as grains of sand
that coddle at the slightest clamour
I count on the child
who will help me get up
to return earth its fertilising
its illusory midnight fruit

Je donnerai tous mes louis d'or
Contre des lingots de bonheur
Pour revivre le temps d'un repentir
Mais la terre ne rejette jamais un semis
Elle en fait des grains de sable
Qui viendront bâtir en poussière
La mémoire dispersée du vent

La lumière de mes yeux s'éteint
Dans son foyer de cendre
Et chaque geste de moi
Est celui d'un autre
Qu'on me met
Pour juguler mon inertie
Et activer la flamme pâle
De mon regard terne

Dans la voiture qui m'amène
À l'asile des âmes
Je surplombe le pont de Colobane
Une marée humaine y vit
Dans des abris de déchets
Au milieu de ferrailles
De détritus et d'odeurs infectes
Où nichent des rats d'égouts
Et des chats de gouttière

Je les envie
Et donnerai tout de moi
Pour leur ravir un instant
De leur misérable vie
De leur vie saine sans artifice
Où chaque instant
Est une prompte fin
Simple et brutale
Comme une bourrasque

I would give all my gold sovereigns
for ingots of happiness
to live again the time to repent
but the earth never rejects a seedling
it turns it into grains of sand
that in the dust will build
the dispersed memory of wind

The light of my eyes dies out
in its hearth of ash
and every gesture I make
is that of another
I am given to wear
to quell my inertia
and kindle the pale flame
of my dulled look

In the car that takes me
to the asylum of souls
I peer down from Colobane bridge
a mass of humanity lives
in shelters made of waste
amidst scrap metal
rubbish and stench
teeming with sewer rats
and feral cats

I envy them
I'd give everything I have
to rob them of a minute
of their miserable life
of their healthy uncomplicated life
where each instant
is a sudden end
simple, brutal
like a squall

Mais la vie me fuit
Et refroidit mes orteils
J'ai peur de perdre
La force des mots
L'énergie tactile de mes sens
J'ai peur d'avoir peur
De finir en grains de sable

À travers les vitres du mobile
J'aperçois des enfants qui jouent
L'air jovial et insouciant
Ils se ruent sur un ballon en chiffon
Leur proie textile
J'agite la main
Pour partager leur joie
Mais mes os craquent
Tel un fagot rongé par les termites
Mon corps se referme alors
M'installant à l'infini
Dans le silence et la nuit

Le Lit de Sable (L'Harmattan, 1998)

But life shuns me
makes my toes cold
I'm afraid of losing
the force of words
the tactile energy of my senses
I'm afraid of being afraid
of ending up grains of sand

Through the mobile's windows
I see happy, carefree
children playing
charging at a rag ball
their cloth prey
I wave
I want to share their joy
but my bones crack
bundle of sticks eaten away by termites
my body closes up
settles me in infinity
in silence and night

AMADOU LAMINE SALL

PHOTO: V. SREENIVASAMURTHY

AMADOU LAMINE SALL lives in Senegal. He has been honoured with the Grand Prix of the Académie française and is widely published in Africa, France, Germany and Canada. His most recent book, *Le Rêve du Bambou*, was published by Éditions Feu de brousse in 2010. *Kamandalu: Selected Poems* translated by Lydie and Jim Haenlin, was published by the Wells College Press. Amadou Lamine Sall is the founder and president of the Maison de la Poésie in Dakar and director of Les Éditions Feu de brousse. As an adviser to the Minister of Culture in Senegal, he works to promote poetry and the arts in schools and oversees the realisation of the Gorée Memorial Project, a UNESCO-sponsored memorial to the African diaspora during the slave trade.

MON PAYS N'EST PAS UN PAYS MORT

"Chacun ici est un héros
avant de naître."
                        PABLO NÉRUDA

    Mon pays n'est pas un baobab nocturne
une herbe noire une fleur froide
un fruit anémique une terre agenouillée
    Mon pays n'est pas une route coupée
une chaussée pourrie un ciel boueux
    Mon pays n'est pas dans l'urgence des vautours
il est dans la foulée des tigres et
le lion a encore la mâchoire qui brûle et le ventre en flammes
    Mon pays n'est pas un pays mort
mais elle est pourtant morte la mémoire
mort le sang dans la case des hommes pressés
et le rêve de ceux qui ont cru dompter l'alphabet court nu dans les rues
et les enfants ne jettent même plus des pierres à ce lambeau de rêve...
    Mon pays n'est mort que dans la hâte de ceux qui marchent
sur les chemins de mirage les yeux glauques l'horizon cupide
    Mon pays n'est mort que dans les fils de l'impatience
les fils malicieux de la politique les sidéens du pouvoir dans
la malaria et le paludisme des urnes
les fils arqués de la politique les bergers à venir mais si fatigués déjà
                                         comme de vieilles
peugeot des années de jazz
    Mon pays n'est mort que dans les rois de midi et
les princes des oracles qui mûrissent le trône en
eux avant le maïs et l'arachide
les terrasses d'or avant la paille de chaume des toits du Sine
la chaise de satin avant le tabouret de termitière
    Mon pays n'est mort que dans les fils surdoués des feux de brousse
qui dévorent jusqu'aux refuges des lépreux aux portails fastes
                                                des banques
    Ce pays mon pays n'est mort que chez les morts d'avant les lampes
car elles arrivent elles arrivent les grandes lampes
arrivent les fauteuils de soie les canapés de laine
dans les taudis des banlieues
arrivent les rideaux rouges et pourpres
arrivent les bronzes rares les toiles des enfants d'Oussouye
les livres des enfants du Fouta
arrivent les sourates les chants grégoriens les libations

MY COUNTRY IS NOT A DEAD COUNTRY

"Everyone here is a hero
before they are born."
PABLO NERUDA

My country is not a nocturnal baobab
blackened grass a cold flower
anaemic fruit a land on its knees
My country is not a road cut off
a pot-holed road surface a muddy sky
My country is not the pressing need of vultures
it is close on the heels of tigers and
the lion still has a burning jaw and fiery belly
My country is not a dead country
yet its memory is dead
and the blood in the men's hut those in a hurry
dead the dream of those who believed they'd tamed the alphabet
run naked in the streets
and children no longer even throw stones at this shred of a dream...
My country is only dead in the haste of those who walk
the paths of a dull-eyed mirage the cupid horizon
My country is only dead among the sons of impatience
the malicious sons of politics those crazed with power
amidst the malaria and swamp fever of the urns
the hunchbacked sons of politics the shepherds of the future
so tired already like the old Peugeot of the jazz years
My country is only dead in the kings of high noon and
princes of oracles that ripen thrones within
before corn and peanut
terraces of gold before thatched roofs of the Sine
the satin chair placed before the anthill stool
My country is only dead in the gifted sons of bush fires
that devour everything from leper refuges to the prosperous bank gates
This country my country is only dead among the dead from
before torches
as they are coming they are coming the majestic lamps
the silk armchairs the wool sofas coming
into suburban slums
then come the red and purple curtains
then come the rare bronzes pictures by Oussouye children
books by children from the Fouta
then come the sourates, the Gregorian chants the libations

arrivent les femmes les hommes d'un siècle nouveau
d'un temps d'espérance

    Mon pays n'est pas un pays mort
malgré les fourmis et les fatigues les cafards
les sommeils lents les réveils taraudés
les souliers usés les chaussettes soumises aux
faims des rats les orteils au vent
    Mon pays n'est pas mort
malgré les journaux aux manchettes de fin du monde
l'Afrique décrétée inapte jusqu'à la fin du monde – mais enfin
si enceinte de vergers rares –
la France comptable de sa tendresse et vivant seule son dépit amoureux
l'Amérique la frousse pleine les yeux mais triomphant dans l'acier de ses bras
    Mon pays n'est pas un pays mort
malgré les cuisines vides dans la solitude d'un oignon
d'une pomme de terre verdâtre comme d'un méchant quolibet
    Mon pays n'est pas un pays mort
une cargaison puante mais une marée haute d'épices et d'encens
il vit ce pays se tourne et se retourne et danse et pleure et chante
dans l'angoisse pourtant infinie que masse une foi infinie
que consolent une cloche un minaret le regard velouté d'une
                                                   maman infinie
    Mon pays n'est pas un pays défunt
il ne porte comme la vie que les pas lourds d'un soldat endeuillé
d'un enfant amputé
comme la vie le sourire au gingembre d'une femme que la beauté honore
il est bien debout mon pays grave beau et fort
    Mais il est vrai que les fleurs si belles meurent
toujours un soir ou est-ce un matin je ne sais plus…
reste alors le parfum qu'elles ont laissé
mais puisse ce parfum habiter la nostalgie des cœurs irriguer le vertige
être le remontoir de nos sens de nos vies nourrir l'avenir sinon
sinon elles seront vraiment mortes les fleurs mortes pour toujours
mortes pour rien mort aussi le triomphe du jour de gloire
    Et l'oubli monstrueux qui se lève tragique
comme une tendresse décapitée
une malédiction brutale dressée comme une lance…
    Mon pays n'est pas un pays mort mon pays n'est pas un murmure
Son peuple au front d'étoiles et à la bouche de sel
est un océan qui ne s'annonce plus
une mer haute féconde navigable pour toutes les fraternités du monde
    Chacun sait ici pour quoi alors nous serons toujours vivants

(unpublished)

then come the women the men of a new century
of a time of hope

    My country is not a dead country
despite the ants and fatigue the roaches
the torpor the tormented awaking
worn shoes socks subjected
to hungry rats toes sticking out
    My country is not dead
despite the papers with end-of-the-world-is-nigh headlines
Africa is declared inapt right up to the end of the world – but still
so fertile with rare orchards –
France is declared accountable for its affection and living alone unrequited love
America's eyes scared shitless but triumphant in its steely grasp
    My country is not a dead country
despite empty kitchens in the solitude of an onion
of a greenish potato as well as a malicious gibe
    My country is not a dead country
a stinking cargo but a high tide of spice and incense
it is alive this country turns & turns over & dances & weeps & sings
in infinite anguish massaged by infinite faith
consoled by a bell a minaret the soft look of an infinite mother
    My country is not defunct
as life it bears only the heavy steps of a mourning soldier
of an amputated child
as life the ginger smile of a woman honoured for her beauty
it is in fine fettle upright my solemn beautiful and strong country
    True such beautiful flowers always die
of an evening or a morning, I can't remember...
there is just the fragrance they left behind
may this fragrance fill the nostalgia of hearts irrigate the vertigo
be the winder of our senses for our lives nourish the future if not
if not they will really be dead flowers forever dead
dead for nothing and the triumph the day of glory will also be dead
    And the monstrous lapse of memory that rises up as tragic
as affection beheaded
a brutal curse erected like a lance...
    My country is not a dead country my country is not a mere whisper
its people with star-studded foreheads and mouths of salt
its people an ocean that no longer approaches
fecund high seas navigable for all the brotherhoods of the world
    Everyone here knows why we will still be alive

TUNISIA

TAHAR BEKRI

TAHAR BEKRI was born in near Gabès, Tunisia, in 1951. He has lived in Paris since 1976. Writing in both French and Arabic, he has published around twenty books of poetry, essays and artists' books. Considered to be one of the leading voices of contemporary North African literature, Tahar Bekri is Maître de Conférences at Université de Paris X-Nanterre. His work, marked by exile, wandering and travels, evokes the continual reinvention of cultures. His essays include *De la littérature tunisienne et maghrébine* (1999) and his poetry collections of note *Le Chant du roi errant, Les songes impatients* and, most recently, *Je te nomme Tunisie* (2011).

AFGHANISTAN

Si la musique doit mourir
Si l'amour est œuvre de Satan
Si ton corps est ta prison
Si le fouet est ce que tu sais donner
Si ton cœur est ta barbe
Si ta vérité est un voile
Si ton refrain est une balle
Si ton chant est oraison funèbre
Si ton faucon est un corbeau
Si ton regard est frère de la poussière

Comment peux-tu aimer le soleil dans ta tanière?

Si ton ciel n'aime guère les cerfs-volants
Si ta terre est un champ de mines
Si ton vent est alourdi par la poudre
Et non par le pollen fécond
Si ton mûrier est une potence
Si ta porte est un barrage
Si ton lit est une tranchée
Si ta maison est un cercueil
Si ton fleuve coule de sang
Si ta neige est un cimetière

Comment peux-tu aimer l'eau dans la rivière?

Si tes montagnes courbent l'échine
Humiliées sans hauteur
Leurs dos pour les injustes citadelles
Leurs boyaux éventrés pour endurcir la pierre
Si ta vallée n'est pas pour nourrir ton rêve
Comme une rose dans le zéphyr
Si ton argile est pétrie de deuils
Non pas pour élever une école
Comme un abricotier en fleurs
Si ton roseau n'est pas un calame

Comment peux-tu habiter la lumière?

AFGHANISTAN

If music were to die
If love is the work of Satan
If your body is your prison
If the whip is what you know how to wield
If your heart is your beard
If your truth is a veil
If your refrain is a bullet
If your song is a funeral prayer
If your falcon is a crow
If your look is brother to dust

How can you love the sun in your lair?

If your sky detests kites
If your soil is a minefield
If your wind is thickened by powder
And not fecund pollen
If your mulberry tree is a gallows
If your door is a barrage
If your bed is a trench
If your house is a coffin
If your river flows with blood
If your snow is a cemetery

How can you love the water in the river?

If your mountains submit
Humiliated and humbled
Their backs unjust citadels
Their guts disembowelled to harden stone
If your valley is not to fuel your dream
Like a rose in the zephyr
If your clay is kneaded by grief
Not to raise a school
Like an apricot tree in flower
If your reed is not a qalam

How can you live in the light?

Si ton labour est semailles d'épouvantails
Une cache lâche pour les pavots
Si ton cheval est esclave de tes œillères
Méprise la course des flûtes dans les airs
Si ta vallée vomit ses saphirs
Aux seigneurs de la guerre
Si les tresses des femmes sont des cordes
Si ton stade est un abattoir
Si ton chemin est invisible
Si ta nuit est une tombe pour les étoiles

Comment peux-tu promettre la lune?

Si Gengis Khan est ton maître
Si ton enfant est graine de Tamerlan
Si ton visage est sans visage
Si ton sabre est ton bourreau
Si ton épopée est ruines et vautours
Si toute la pluie ne peut laver ton index
Si ton désir est un bois mort
Si ton feu est cendre
Si ta flamme est fumée
Si ta passion est grenades et canons

Comment peux-tu séduire la colombe à ta fenêtre?

Si ton village est une caserne
Non un nid pour les hirondelles
Si ta maison est une caverne
Si ta source est un mirage
Si ton habit est ton linceul
Si la mort est ton mausolée
Si ton Coran est un turban
Si ta prière est une guerre
Si ton paradis est enfer
Si ton âme est ta sombre geôlière

Comment peux-tu aimer le printemps?

Si la musique doit mourir (Ed. Al Manar, Paris, 2006)

If your labour is seed for scarecrows
Craven cache for poppies
If your horse is enslaved by its blinkers
Scorns the flight of flutes in the air
If your valley vomits its sapphires
To the warlords
If the braids of women are ropes
If your stadium is a slaughterhouse
If your path is invisible
If your night is a tomb for the stars

How can you promise the moon?

If Gengis Khan is your master
If your child is the offspring of Timur
If your face is faceless
If your sabre is your executioner
If your epic is ruins and vultures
If all the rain cannot wash your forefinger
If your desire is dead wood
If your fire is ash
If your flame is smoke
If your passion is grenades and cannon

How can you seduce the dove at the window?

If your village is a casern
Not a nest for swallows
If your house is a cave
If your source is a mirage
If your dress is your shroud
If death is your mausoleum
If your Koran is a turban
If your prayer is war
If your paradise is hell
If your soul is your sombre gaoler

How can you love the spring?

OMBRE

Le rêve comme marron sur braise
Fugitif la poudre à ses trousses
Ni les océans n'abritent son attente
Ni les flamboyants ne le consolent
Jour après jour les brûlures
Enchaînent au silence ses impatiences

Elle seule l'ombre sait étreindre
La froide et brûlante larme
Sur la joue de la nuit écarlate
Par-delà les frontières
Par-delà les aurores boréales
Corps à corps les captifs se souviennent

Marcher sur l'oubli (Editions L'Harmattan, 2000)

SONGE À TRIESTE

Te revoilà vieille mer
Remplie de mes ancres
Ni la vague absente
Ni le silence de la lumière
Ne disent à la mouette
Sois douce
Pour mes voiles
Combien de rides
Cordes offertes à l'errance
Faut-il au soleil
Pour être sourd aux canons
Voici mes mâts
Jalousant les insouciants sapins
Plus inquiets que les collines
De trop aimer les clochers
Sarajevo brûle
Que n'as-tu aboli les frontières
Dans les veines du vent

SHADE

The dream like a marron on hot coals
a fugitive the powder hot on his heels
the oceans do not shelter its waiting
nor do the flamboyants console it
day after day the burns
chain up this impatience in silence

Only the shade knows how to embrace
the cold burning tear
on the cheek of the scarlet night
beyond the frontiers
beyond the northern lights
hand-to-hand the captives remember

DREAM AT TRIESTE

Here you are again old sea
full of my anchors
neither the absent wave
nor the silence of the light
tell the seagull
be gentle
to my sails
how many wrinkles
ropes offered up to wandering
does the sun need
to be deaf to the cannons
here are my masts
jealous of the carefree pines
and more troubled than the hills
we keep loving the bell towers too much
Sarajevo is burning
why have you not abolished the frontiers
in the veins of the wind

Ulysse
Aux secrètes amours
Dérobées à l'horizon

Te revoilà épuisée mer
Des pas alourdis
Sur les quais
Ni le port
N'a ravi les corsaires
Ni la pierre
N'a sauvé les neiges
Les souvenirs
Portés par les écumes
Le sel blesse leurs ailes
La nuit vole leurs vols
Cime après cime
Tu crains les aigles
Leurs griffes comme des balles
Dans les brumes sonores
Que n'as-tu imploré les rochers
La désinvolte hirondelle
Mer meurtrie
Pour étreindre la frivole eau
Dans les bras du soir écarlate
Et éteindre tous ces incendies

Marcher sur l'oubli (Editions L'Harmattan, 2000)

LE PÊCHEUR DE LUNES

I

Il marchait
Sur la lune
    Les planètes à l'envi de glace
    À moi les étoiles tout l'univers
    Demain au fond de la terre
    Criait-il aux forêts disparues

    Je régnerai sur tous les déserts

Ulysses
with your secret loves
lifted from the horizon

Here you are again exhausted sea
heavy footsteps
on the quays
the port has not
ravished the corsairs
nor the stone
saved the snows
the memories
borne away by the foam
the salt wounds their wings
the night steals their flights
peak after peak
you fear the eagles
their claws like bullets
in the resonant mists
why have you not implored the rocks
the casual swallow
and the bruised sea
to embrace the frivolous water
in the arms of the scarlet evening
and put out all these fires

THE FISHERMAN OF MOONS

I

He walked
On the moon
      The planets vying him with ice
      The stars, the whole universe, it's all mine
      Tomorrow deep down in the earth
      He shouted out to vanished forests

      I will reign over all the deserts

II

Je croiserai
Les océans
    Et leur dirai la lave des volcans
    Peu importe si les fossiles
    Méprisent mon vieux squelette
    Parmi les phosphates tyranniques

    L'eau se souviendra des cours de l'or

III

Peu importe
Si les jours
    Se rient de mes pétales désemparés
    Ils conteront aux coraux
    Leurs pourpres frissons
    Les aiguilles comme des soupirs

    Rapiècent le rêve aux cheveux blancs

IV

C'est Mars
Que j'arrache
    À ton sommeil dans les fougères
    Te dirai-je comment
    Les vents ont emporté tant d'amis
    Les tilleuls remèdes à l'éphémère

    Dans la nuit si brève les calvaires

V

Sous les pas
De poussière
    Insolentes les bottes rasaient
    Tes coquelicots
    Que n'ai-je dit au creux de ta main

II

I will meet
The oceans
      And tell them of volcanic lava
      It doesn't matter if the fossils
      Despise my old skeleton
      Among the tyrannical phosphates

      The water will remember the price of gold

III

It doesn't matter
If the days
      Laugh at my helpless petals
      They will tell the coral
      Of their purple shivers
      The needles like sighs

      Patch up the white-haired dream

IV

I drag Mars
Out
      Of your sleep among the ferns
      Will I tell you how
      The winds bore away so many friends
      Lime tree remedies for the ephemeral

      In such a brief night the calvaries

V

Under the footsteps
of dust
      Insolent the boots razed
      Your poppies
      What didn't I say to the palm of your hand

Sois dans la prompte lumière rivière

Ou colombe pour les ciels outragés

VI

Combien
D'oliviers
  Faut-il à mes os poudreux
  Pour dérober
  À tes rochers leurs bruyères
  Aux feux leurs étincelles

  De tant de mers l'écume vengeresse

VII

Dans la ville
Empaillée
  Il déclarait la fin du paysage
  Ici les cimetières ont des étages
  Les gratte-ciel confondaient
  Hirondelles et libres nuages

  Le long des murs les herbes folles

Le pêcheur de lunes [artists' book] (Editions Bernard Lafabrie)

Be river in the swift light

Or a dove for outraged skies

VI

How many
Olive trees
    Do my powdery bones need
    To steal
    The heather from your rocks
    The sparks from fires

    Foam vengeful of so many seas

VII

In the straw-stuffed
Town
    He declared the end of the countryside
    Here the cemeteries have storeys
    The skyscrapers muddled
    Swallows with free-floating clouds

    Along the walls the grasses are wild

SHAMS NADIR

SHAMS NADIR is the pseudonym of Tunisian poet and novelist Mohammed Aziza, born in 1940. Mohammed Aziza started out as a director of Tunisian Radio-TV, and subsequently became an international civil servant with UNESCO in Paris. His writing has been appreciated for its depth and originality by leading men of letters worldwide such as Julio Cortasar and Léopold Sédor Senghor, which earned him the post of Rector of the Euro-Arab Itinerant University. Through the guise of a pseudonym, Aziza wishes to create a dividing line between his work as poet and novelist and his aesthetic essays on the status of art in Arab-Islamic civilization. The latter include at least six essays in which he re-examines the problem of 'Muslim iconoclasm' and highlights the richness and variety of Islamic plastic arts. The author's inspiration is not the quest of origins but the quest of origin, 'the first breath' of mankind.

L'AUTRE SINDABAD (extraits)

I

Une masque m'échut aux prémisses du monde
Et mes cendres délébiles ont, longtemps, crissé
    au fond des tophets puniques.
Et mon souffle impuissant s'épuisa, longtemps,
    aux frontons de la gloire romaine.
O ma sève, ma sève numide.
Toujours, il y eut l'errance et toujours le vent.
Et l'exultation des sables en vaines armées de cristaux.
Et l'abri humide des cavernes au flanc des steppes
    de l'exil.
Et toujours la nudité des touffes, au creux
    de l'été proféré.
Toujours, toujours le rêve
    tenace et fragile
D'une rive où aborder pour renaître
Nu et réconcilié
et vivant
    au rythme des palmes balancées.

II

O ma sève, ma sève numide
Comment te traquer au mystère de toute chair naissante
Comment te reconnaître au travers de la forêt pétrifiée
des signes illicites
Comment retrouver ta trace profonde, quand me vrille
l'empreinte du Faux.
Si je venais à arracher mon masque
Ma chair partirait en lambeaux.

III

Clameur de l'exil au rivage des Syrtes!
Le temps est venu de déserter ce jardin du mirage.
Sur trop de mensonges, je m'étais assoupi
De trop d'ossuaires, je m'étais amusé.
Sur les grèves de rocailles et d'amiante,

THE OTHER SINDBAD (extracts)

   I

A mask left me stranded at the beginnings of the world
and my delible ashes for a long while swirled
   in the depths of Punic Tophets.
And my powerless breath wore itself out, for a long time
   at the pediments of Roman glory.
O my life-blood, my Numidian vigour.
There has always been roaming, always the wind
And the exultation of sands as vain armies of crystal.
And the damp shelter of hillside caves in the steppes
   of exile.
And bare tufts, always there, in the hollow
   of a summer brought forth.
Always, always, the tenacious, fragile
   dream
Of a river bank where to land is to be reborn
Naked, reconciled
and living
at the pace of swaying palm trees.

   II

O my life-blood, my Numidian vigour
How can I track you down to the mystery of nascent flesh
How can I recognise you through the petrified forest
   of illicit signs
How can I find your deep-rooted trace again, twisted as I am
by the mark of Falsehood.
If I wrenched off my mask
My flesh would fall into shreds.

   III

The clamour of exile on the shores of Surt!
The time has come to desert this garden of mirages.
I was lulled by so many lies,
Amused by so many charnel houses.
On stone strewn shores, asbestos-laden strand,

L'oiseau des îles a terni son somptueux plumage
et la jungle malhabile a banni la résurgence des eaux.
      Alors j'ai déployé mes voiles
      Aux vents des départs.
      Laboure, ô proue, le champ fertile
      Où rêvent les méduses.
      Jaillissent l'embrun et la tornade sous-marine
      et les spasmes de l'éclair.
      À grandes eaux salées
      Lavez mes yeux d'un songe trop vivace

      O trombes des profondeurs.

    IV

Nous avions rendez-vous avec l'Aube.
    Sur l'autre versant des monts bâtés de neige
    Comme un chargement de pétales blanches.
    Sur l'autre rive du Fleuve, au portail du Songe
    La où palpite, clarté sans torche,
    La rose noire du Signe.

    V

Nous avions rendez-vous avec l'Aube.
    Sous les griffes du vent, sous l'étirement du soir
    Nous devancions nos ombres
    Interrogeant, sans cesse, les osselets de nos Mages
    Retraçant les pictogrammes de nos Tablettes
    Psalmodiant nos formules rituelles.

    [...]

    XXIX

Au cadran de l'astrolabe, le présent chavire...
      C'était une belle flottille
            avant que d'être décimée...
      Ici, une frégate nommée liberté
           coule dans un hoquêtement furieux.

The Caribbean bird dulled its sumptuous plumage
and the clumsy jungle banished the resurgence of water.
    So I unfurled my sails
    before the winds of departure.
    Plough, O prow, the fertile field
    Where jellyfish dream.
    Seadrift, subsea tornado
    and lightning spasms gush forth.
    Douse my eyes with ocean water
    To wash away an overly quick dream

    O torrents of the depths.

    IV

We arranged to meet the Dawn.
    On the other slope of mountains packsaddled with snow
    A load of white petals.
    On the other bank of the River, at the gateway of Dream
    Where there flickers, in torchless daylight,
    The black rose of the Sign.

    V

We arranged to meet the Dawn
    Under the wind's claws, the evening as it stretches
    We preceded our shadows
    Ceaselessly questioning the jacks of our Magi
    Recounting the pictographs of our Tablets
    Chanting our ritual formulae.

    [...]

    XXIX

On the face of the astrolabe, the present keels over...
    It was a beautiful flotilla
        before it was decimated...
    Here a frigate named freedom
        sinks with almighty hiccoughing.

>   Là, une caravelle nommée
>   Astrologie
>   ou médecine
>   ou algèbre
>   ou philosophie
>   s'anéantit dans les miasmes aqueux.

Ici et là,

Le vert glauque et froid des eaux profondes
>   M'étreint
>   Me noie
Quand donc finirai-je de sombrer?

>   xxx

Il est temps de rêver…

>   Sur le mat de misaine
>   J'amène l'étendard de ma raison
>   Et je surgis de l'onde
>   Et je marche sur les eaux
>   À ta recherche, Imam Caché
>   Prophète Masqué
>   Je marche.

Nous verdirons les terres rougies de Canaan
Nous t'ensemencerons, ventre stérile de Sehna
Et nous inventerons un temps sans mémoire
>   pour rompre le pain sous les tentes de Kédar
>   pour faire pousser la vigne au flanc de l'Hermon et de l'Atlas
>   pour inscrire la renaissance aux patois de notre durée

Et nous inventerons un lieu sans enclos
>   pour rassembler les frères reconnus
>   pour rendre à la cité la liberté du dire et du penser
>   pour bannir le temps des loups
>   Nous TENTERONS
>   d'accomplir le règne des mains jointes
>   et des cœurs accordés

Et que sur le mât de misaine
Flotte l'étendard de notre espérance

L'Athanor (Editions L'Harmattan, 2001)

>   Over there a caravel called
>   Astrology
>   or medicine
>   or algebra
>   or philosophy
>   vanishes utterly in aqueous miasma

Here and there,

The glaucous cold of the deep
>   Embraces me
>   Drowns me
When will I ever cease to founder?

           xxx

It is time to dream...

>   I bring the standard of my reason
>   To the foresail mast
>   And I surge out of the deep
>   And I walk on water
>   In search of you, Occulted Iman
>   masked prophet
>   I walk.
We will turn the red earth of Canaan green
We will seed you, barren belly of Selma
And we will invent a time that has no memory
>   to break bread under the tents of Kedar
>   to grow vines on the slopes of Mount Hermon and Atlas
>   to inscribe renaissance on the inner walls of our time here
And we will invent a place without enclosure
>   to assemble recognized brothers
>   to restore freedom of speech and thought to the city
>   to banish the time of wolves
>   We will ENDEAVOUR
>   to accomplish the reign of joined hands
>   and hearts in accord
And from the foresail mast
We shall fly our standard of hope

ECHOS DE L'ISLA-NEGRA
À la mémoire de Pablo Neruda

"Allons poème d'amour, lève toi d'entre ce verre brisé,
car l'heure est venue de chanter."
Pablo Neruda, Memoires
('J'avoue que j'ai vécu')

Sans désir autre que la femme aux cheveux d'écumes
    Ondulant sous ma main sargasse
Sans désir autre que ses yeux de lichen
    Dévoilant les simulacres de la mer
Sans désir autre que ses lèvres de corail
    Faisant cabrer les hippocampes
Sans désir autre que son corps
    Dune s'alimentant aux sources les plus secrètes du vent
Sans désir autre que l'union
    Ressac des marées sous la pâmoison des lunes pleines
Sans désir autre que la perdition
    Dans les nécropoles de sable, aux alluvions de la nuit
Sans désir autre que la résurrection
    Sous la neige de l'amandier, aux embouchures de l'aube.

(Unpublished)

ECHOES OF ISLA NEGRA
for Pablo Neruda

"Come on love poem, lift yourself up from
among this broken glass, the time has come to sing."
PABLO NERUDA, *Memoirs*
('Confieso que he vivido')

Desiring only the woman with hair of sea foam
    Rippling under my gulfweed hands
Desiring only her lichen eyes
    Revealing the semblance of the sea
Desiring only her lips of coral
    Making seahorses rear
Desiring only her body
    Dune nourished by the wind's innermost sources
Desiring only union
    Undertow of tides enraptured by full moons
Desiring only perdition
    In the burial yards of sand, alluvial sediment of night
Desiring only resurrection
    Under the snow of almond trees, in estuaries of dawn

AMINA SAÏD

AMINA SAÏD was born in Tunisia in 1953. She teaches English literature in Paris. One of the leading Arab women poets writing in French, Amina Saïd has published around a dozen collections of poetry and translated Philippine writer Francisco Sionil José from English. Her work was the subject of *Convergences et fractures de deux mondes, l'Orient et l'Occident chez Amina Saïd* (University of Bari, Italy, 1995). She received the Prix Jean Malrieu in 1989 for *Feu d'oiseaux* and Prix Charles-Vildrac from the Société des gens de lettres in 1994 for her poetry collection *L'une et l'autre nuit*. Her most recent collections are *L'absence l'inachevé* (Editions de La Différence, 2009) and *Les saisons d'Aden* (Al Manar, Neuilly, 2011).

* * *

chaque jour le soleil égorge son spectre
et se lève dans son sang

tout commencement dessine un cercle
la mémoire mène à la mer des commencements
la jetée est de pierre l'arbre d'exil
j'aspire à l'horizon

sur un fil de lumière
je vais vers ce lieu qui est toi
et ce qui fut advient

une étoile danse sur le ciel de mon front
l'oiseau en nous renaît de la rive de l'âme
ta parole est tienne mienne est ma parole

tu rejoins le lieu que je suis
et le poème continue de s'écrire

nous sommes la pierre et le chant
le silence intense l'ombre le rêve et la distance
de nous-même à nous-même

je vois ton visage et l'ombre sur ton visage
comme le poème la souffrance se partage
nous compatissons à l'arbre, aux saisons
trop brèves et à l'exil des saisons
aux sourires et aux déchirements de la terre
aux malheurs des hommes aux prières des femmes

à nos vœux l'instant prend sa forme éblouie
le temps s'efface tel un paysage
nous vivons les deux moitiés de nos vies
comme un voyage qui se souviendrait peut-être
du nom des îles des oiseaux des ports
du sillage blanc des navires des villes des êtres
du cycle des arrivées et des départs

et nous tombons amoureux de la nuit
parce que chaque nuit célèbre les noces du rêve

* * *

each day the sun slits its spectre's throat
and rises in a pool of blood

every beginning draws a circle
memory leads to the sea of beginnings
the pier is made of stone the tree of exile
I seek the horizon

on a thread of light
I go towards this place that is you
and what was comes to pass

a star dances on the sky of my forehead
the bird within rises from the banks of the soul
your word is yours mine is my word

you reach the place that I am
and the poem continues to be written

we are stone and song
deep silence shadow dream and distance
from ourselves to ourselves

I see your face and the shadow on your face
as with the poem suffering is shared
we commiserate with the tree, with seasons
that are all too brief and with the exile of seasons
with smiles and rifts in the earth
with the misfortune of men and prayers of women

by our vows the instant marries its dazzling shape
time is erased like a landscape
we live the two halves of our lives
like a journey that would probably remember
the name of islands birds ports
the white wake of boats towns beings
the cycle of arrivals and departures

and we fall in love with night
because each night celebrates the dream marriage

et nous tombons amoureux du jour
parce que la vie commence avec chaque jour

    * * *

désormais les mères dorment seules
parmi les portraits des morts
elles seules savent où ils s'en sont allés
et comment le long travail du mourir
déjà les séparait du vivant

les mères désormais seules errent
parmi les tombes des défunts
récitant le long des avenues de la mort
des prières en des langues inconnues
égrenant le lourd chapelet du temps écoulé

elles ne comptent plus le temps
aux nuits qui tombent sur la terre
ni aux matins qui se lèvent sur le monde
à tous elles demandent où commencent
où finissent les territoires de la mort

les mères découvrent la solitude
le monde circonscrit à un carre de terre dure
elles refont le même rêve qui entrebâille les ténèbres
conversent avec le vide des miroirs
redisent la même prière où se meurt la lumière du jour

désormais entre les draps défaits du temps
les mères célèbrent leurs noces solitaires
dans le silence profond des maisons
des horloges sans aiguilles
rythment le passage des heures

désormais la nuit a des yeux
qui traquent l'insomnie des mères
en elles habitent les deux anges qui demain
nous demanderont des comptes quand notre tour
viendra d'approcher les portes du ciel

and we fall in love with day
because life begins with each day

         * * *

the mothers sleep alone now
among the portraits of their dead
they alone know where they have gone
and how the long process of dying
already separates them from the living

the mothers alone now wander
among the tombs of the deceased
reciting along the avenues of death
prayers in unknown tongues
telling the heavy beads of time past

they no longer count the hours
to nights that fall over the earth
nor to mornings that rise on the world
to all they ask where begins
and where ends the realm of death

the mothers discover solitude
the world reduced to a square of hard earth
they dream the same dream that leaves darkness ajar
converse with the emptiness of mirrors
repeat the same prayer in which the light of day dies

lying between unmade sheets of time
the mothers celebrate their solitary weddings
in the profound silence of houses
clocks without hands
tick away the hours

the night now has eyes
that track the insomnia of mothers
in whom live the two angels that tomorrow
will ask us to bear account when
it's our turn to stand before heaven's gates

le fil du chapelet rompu
les mères versent l'eau de leurs larmes

dans la coupelle des tombes
elles surveillent le vol des oiseaux
les messages des morts entre leurs ailes

notre seconde demeure se dresse
dans l'avenue de la mort disent les mères
pourquoi avons-nous donné la vie
pour jusqu'à notre dernier souffle
la disputer à l'ombre

des nôtres nous ne voyons qu'os blanchis
les mains souillées de la terre des cimetières
nous plantons arbres et arbustes que leurs branches
soient le toit de leur nouvelle demeure
si seulement nous avions su disent les mères

nous relisons les lettres des défunts
et imaginons des réponses neuves
tout s'éclaire lorsqu'il est trop tard
nous n'avons plus assez du fil des regrets
pour assembler les morceaux de notre nuit

nos mains tremblent disent encore les mères
à contempler de trop profondes ténèbres
nos yeux ne voient presque plus la lumière
les soleils ont déserté nos jardins et les nuages
en de longs haillons gris pendent aux arbres

tous nous dansons accrochés tels des pantins
au bout de la corde du temps
nos gestes sont la réplique
de gestes anciens et personne désormais
n'entend notre parole expropriée

que n'aurions-nous fait pour ceux que nous aimons
ôtant les échardes du bouquet épineux de la vie
puis une à une les roses se sont flétries
désormais depuis le cadre d'une fenêtre
nous contemplons les noces de la mer avec l'horizon

the thread of the rosary is broken
the mothers fill the dishes on the tombs

with the water of their tears
keep a close eye on the flight of birds
messages from the dead between their wings

our second home lies
in the avenues of the dead the mothers say
why did we give life
only to struggle with it in the shade
up to our last breath

of our own we only see whitened bones
hands soiled with the earth of cemeteries
we plant trees and bushes may their branches
be the roof of their new home
if only we had known the mothers say

we reread the letters of the dead
and imagine new replies
it all becomes clear once it's too late
we never have enough threads of sorrow
to patch together the fragments of our night

our hands tremble the mothers say again
from looking at the profound darkness too long
our eyes can barely see the light now
sun has deserted our gardens and clouds
in long grey tatters hang from the trees

we are all dancing like puppets
at the end of the rope of time
our gestures are the replica
of ancient gestures and nobody now
hears our expropriated speech

what wouldn't we have done for those we love
removing the thorns from life's barbed crown
then one by one the roses withered
and now from the windowsill
we watch the sea marry the horizon

notre vie une lueur vacillante environnée d'ombre
peu à peu nous nous défaisons de nos vertèbres
chaque jour courbées davantage
par le poids dérisoire de la mémoire
et par l'attente de notre propre fin

 * * *

depuis le lieu natal
nous répondons à quelque obscur appel

percevoir la lumière dans la clarté
l'infime vibration de l'ombre
la tendresse de l'aube au sortir du labyrinthe
l'ensoleillement d'une parole aventureuse

donner ce que nous avons
et prendre ce qui nous est offert
ce que nous sommes un jour sera

être un avec le monde
habiter les quatre dimensions de l'espace
et l'infini de l'instant /source d'étoiles

raccorder l'arbre à son fruit
la fleur à l'accalmie de son sourire
l'oiseau bariolé aux gammes de son ciel
l'étincelle de la présence aux feux consumants
de l'absence l'astre insoupçonné
à la poudrière de l'humaine mémoire

chercher le sens précis des choses
le visage intérieur de chacun
derrière l'imprononçable de la mort

le temps nous est compté
cheminant dans le vent de la parole
j'attends mon amour / éprouvante joie /
pour de longs départs bleus

our life a wavering light amidst shadows
bit by bit our spines buckle
each day bent over a little more
by the derisory weight of memory
and the wait for our own end

* * *

from our birth place
we answer some obscure call

see light in brightness
the slight vibration of shade
the soft dawn at the mouth of the labyrinth
the sunshine of an adventurous word

give what we have
and take what we are offered
what we are will one day be

one with the world
to live the four dimensions of space
the infinity of an instant / source of stars

join the tree to its fruit
the flower to the lull of its smile
the rainbow-coloured bird to the scales of its sky
the spark of presence to all-consuming fires
of absence the unsuspecting star
to the powder keg of human memory

seek the precise meaning of things
the inner face of every one of us
behind the unpronounceable death

our time is counted
making my way through the winds of speech
I await my love / the nerve-racking joy /
for long blue departures

il est permis de rêver aujourd'hui
le jour est lambeaux de silence
quand le poème ne cesse de dire l'ami l'ailleurs

jamais un lieu

L'Absence l'inachevé (Editions de La Différence, Paris, 2009)

we are allowed to dream today
day is shreds of silence
when the poem keeps on saying friend elsewhere

never the right place

ABOUT THE TRANSLATORS

PATRICK WILLIAMSON was born in Madrid in 1960 and lives near Paris, France. His most recent poetry collections are *Bacon, Bits, & Buriton* (Corrupt Press, 2011), and *Trois Rivières / Three Rivers*, (Editions Harmattan, 2010). He has translated the selected poems of Tunisian poet Tahar Bekri (*Inconnues Saisons / Unknown Seasons*, L'Harmattan, Paris, 1999) and the Quebecois poet Gilles Cyr (*The Graph of Roads*, Guernica Editions, 2008). He is the editor of *Quarante et un poètes de Grande-Bretagne* (Ecrits des Forges / Le Temps de Cerises, 2003).

YANN LOVELOCK lives and works in Birmingham, England. In addition to numerous collections of his own poetry and scholarly work, he has published translations from French, Dutch, Wallon, Flemish, Urdu, Spanish, and Danish and held guest editorships, notably for *Modern Poetry in Translation* Dutch & Flemish issue, 1997. As a Buddhist, he has been widely involved in educational work and inter-faith dialogue.

Other anthologies of poetry in translation
published in bilingual editions
by Arc Publications include:

Altered State: An Anthology of New Polish Poetry
EDS. ROD MENGHAM, TADEUSZ PIÓRO, PIOTR SZYMOR
Translated by Rod Mengham, Tadeusz Pióro *et al*

A Fine Line: New Poetry from Eastern & Central Europe
EDS. JEAN BOASE-BEIER, ALEXANDRA BÜCHLER, FIONA SAMPSON
Various translators

Six Slovenian Poets
ED. BRANE MOZETIC
Translated by Ana Jelnikar, Kelly Lennox Allen
& Stephen Watts, with an introduction by Ales Debeljak
No. 1 in the 'New Voices from Europe & Beyond' anthology series
Series Editor: Alexandra Büchler

Six Basque Poets
ED. MARI JOSE OLAZIREGI
Translated by Amaia Gabantxo,
with an introduction by Mari Jose Olaziregi
No. 2 in the 'New Voices from Europe & Beyond' anthology series,
Series Editor: Alexandra Büchler

Six Czech Poets
ED. ALEXANDRA BÜCHLER
Translated by Alexandra Büchler, Justin Quinn & James Naughton,
with an introduction by Alexandra Büchler
No. 3 in the 'New Voices from Europe & Beyond' anthology series,
Series Editor: Alexandra Büchler

Six Lithuanian Poets
ED. EUGENIJUS ALISANKA
Various translators, with an introduction by Eugenijus Alisanka
No. 4 in the 'New Voices from Europe & Beyond' anthology series,
Series Editor: Alexandra Büchler

Six Polish Poets
ED. JACEK DEHNEL
Various translators, with an introduction by Jacek Dehnel
No. 5 in the 'New Voices from Europe & Beyond' anthology series,
Series Editor: Alexandra Büchler

Six Slovak Poets
ED. IGOR HOCHEL
Translated by John Minahane, with an introduction by Igor Hochel
No. 6 in the 'New Voices from Europe & Beyond' anthology series,
Series Editor: Alexandra Büchler

Six Macedonian Poets
ED. IGOR ISAKOVSKI
Various translators, with an introduction by Ana Martinoska
No. 7 in the 'New Voices from Europe & Beyond' anthology series,
Series Editor: Alexandra Büchler

Six Latvian Poets
ED. IEVA LESINSKA
Various translators, with an introduction by Juris Kronbergs
No. 8 in the 'New Voices from Europe & Beyond' anthology series,
Series Editor: Alexandra Büchler

A Balkan Exchange: Eight Poets from Bulgaria & Britain
ED. W. N. HERBERT

The Page and The Fire: Poems by Russian Poets on Russian Poets
ED. PETER ORAM
Selected, translated and introduced by Peter Oram

New Order – Hungarian Poets of the post 1989 Generation
ED. GEORGE SZIRTES
Various translators, with an introduction by George Szirtes